MY FIRST BRITANNICA

The Americas

9

ENCYCLOPÆDIA

Britannica®

CHICAGO   LONDON   NEW DELHI   PARIS   SEOUL   SYDNEY   TAIPEI   TOKYO

International Standard Book Number: 1-59339-048-3 (set)
International Standard Book Number: 1-59339-057-2 (volume 9)

My First Britannica:
Volume 9: The Americas 2004

Britannica.com may be accessed on the Internet at http://www.britannica.com.

The Americas

TABLE OF CONTENTS

The Americas

INTRODUCTION

Who built Machu Picchu?
Why is the United States called a melting pot?
What's an isthmus? How does the Panama Canal work?

In Volume 9,
The Americas,

you'll discover answers to these questions and many more. Through pictures, articles, and fun facts, you'll learn about many of the countries and cities of North, Central, and South America.

To help you on your journey, we've provided the following signposts in *The Americas*:

■ **Subject Tabs**—The coloured box in the upper corner of each right-hand page will quickly tell you the article subject.

■ **Search Lights**—Try these mini-quizzes before and after you read the article and see how much - *and how quickly* - you can learn. You can even make this a game with a reading partner. (Answers are upside down at the bottom of one of the pages.)

■ **Did You Know?**—Check out these fun facts about the article subject. With these surprising 'factoids', you can entertain your friends, impress your teachers, and amaze your parents.

■ **Picture Captions**—Read the captions that go with the photos. They provide useful information about the article subject.

■ **Vocabulary**—New or difficult words are in **bold type**. You'll find them explained in the Glossary at the back of this volume. And there's a complete listing of all Glossary terms in the set in the **Reference Guide and Index**, Volume 13.

■ **Learn More!**—Follow these pointers to related articles throughout the set.

■ **Maps**—You'll find lots of information in this volume's many maps.

■ The **Country Maps** point out national capitals. **Globes** beside Subject Tabs show where countries are located in the world.

■ The **Continent Maps** have a number key showing the location of all countries.

■ The **Icons** on the maps highlight major geographic features and climate. Here's a key to what the map icons mean:

☀ Deserts and Other Dry Areas

❄ Polar Regions and Other Frozen Areas

⛰ Mountains

🌴 Rainforests

🌳 General Forests

■ The **Mini-Atlas**, found in Volume 13, offers detailed maps, useful data tables, and assorted photographs of each continent.

And don't forget: If you're not sure where to start, where you saw something before, or where to go next, the *Reference Guide and Index* (Volume 13) will point the way.

Gold funerary mask of the South American Chimú Indians
© Gianni Dagli Orti/Corbis

Have a great trip!

MY FIRST BRITANNICA

COUNTRIES OF NORTH AMERICA

1. Canada
2. Greenland
3. Mexico
4. United States
5. West Indies
6. Central America*

*Countries of Central America are Belize, Costa Rica, El Salvador, Guatemala, Honduras, Nicaragua, and Panama (*see* page 44)
U.S. state of Hawaii off map

Morning light on Mount Rushmore, South Dakota, U.S.
© Paul A. Souders/Corbis

Dzoonokwa Totem Pole in Thunderbird Park, Victoria, British Columbia, Canada.
© Gunter Marx Photography/Corbis

Land of Plenty

SEARCH LIGHT

North America is the third largest continent. Three countries - Canada, the United States, and Mexico - make up most of it. The countries of Central America are also usually considered part of North America. They occupy a narrow strip of land that connects North America to South America. Several islands, including Greenland in the north and the West Indies in the south, are part of North America too.

Because it's so large, the continent has many different types of climate. Most of Greenland is covered with ice all the time - even in summer. But the southern islands and countries are usually hot and humid. In between there are both deserts and rainy areas, but most places have warm summers and cold winters.

North America is rich in **natural resources**. Forests cover a large part of the land. The **fertile** soils of Canada, the United States, and Mexico produce large amounts of maize, cotton, soybeans, tobacco, wheat, and other crops. The continent is also rich in minerals such as coal, iron ore, copper, natural gas, **petroleum**, and silver.

The history of the continent goes back thousands of years. Scientists believe that people from Asia crossed over to Alaska more than 20,000 years ago and then moved southward. Their **descendants** eventually established great civilizations, such as that of the Maya in Central America and the Aztec in Mexico. The first Europeans in the region were the Vikings, who settled in Greenland in about the 900s. It wasn't until 1492 that explorers from other parts of Europe began to arrive.

According to scientists, who were the first people to settle in North America?
a) Africans
b) Europeans
c) Asians

LEARN MORE! READ THESE ARTICLES…
CENTRAL AMERICA (VOLUME 9) • CONTINENTS (VOLUME 1)
EUROPE (VOLUME 6)

DID YOU KNOW?
More dinosaur fossils have been found in North America than on any other continent.

Answer: c) Asians

Frozen Island

 Greenland is the world's largest island. It sits in the North Atlantic Ocean between Iceland (to the east) and the islands of the Canadian north (to the west). Most of Greenland lies within the Arctic Circle. Its northern tip is only 800 kilometres from the North Pole. The capital city is Nuuk.

Greenland is almost entirely covered in ice. In some places the ice is 3,000 metres thick. Some of the ice is so deep that it is actually below the level of the sea around the island. The people live on the seacoast highlands that are free of ice. Greenland's open land is called '**tundra**'. It has very few trees, and grasses, grass-like plants called 'sedges', and moss-like lichens are the main plants.

The weather in Greenland is cold and may change quickly from sunshine to blizzards. Normal winter temperatures are –6°C in the south and –33°C in the north. Even in the warmest parts of the island, summer temperatures hover around 7°C.

Aside from people, only seven kinds of **mammals** brave Greenland's cold weather on land. They are polar bears, musk oxen, reindeer, arctic foxes, snow hares, ermines, and lemmings. Seals and whales gather in the ocean waters, and Greenlanders once depended on them for food. Nowadays they are more likely to fish for cod, salmon, flounder, and halibut.

Most Greenlanders are of Inuit (Eskimo) **heritage**. They moved there from North America between 4000 BC and AD 1000. In the early 1700s Denmark **colonized** Greenland, and the Danes still control it today.

LEARN MORE! READ THESE ARTICLES…
DENMARK (VOLUME 6) • ISLANDS (VOLUME 1)
VIKINGS (VOLUME 4)

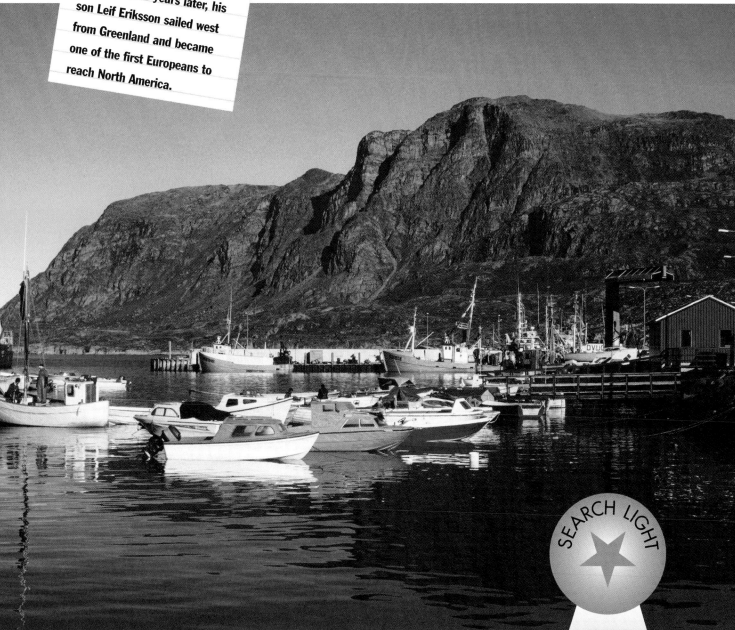

Fishing boats are moored in a harbour in Sisimiut, Greenland.
© Deanna Swaney/Lonely Planet Images

SEARCH LIGHT

Most of Greenland's surface is covered by
a) rice.
b) ice.
c) trees.

Answer: b) ice.

The Land of Long Winters

Canada is the second largest country in the world in terms of land size, after Russia. But it has fewer people than many other countries that are much smaller. This is because much of Canada is a very cold place with long winters. In the northern islands it is often freezing cold even in summer.

Canada has a low **population** for its size. It is one of the world's wealthier countries. Much of the country's wealth lies in its many mines and forests. Minerals such as coal, copper, nickel, and iron ore are found in the mines. Farming is also very important. Canada grows a large amount of grain. It sells a lot of wheat and other products to other countries.

Most Canadians live in towns and cities. Toronto is the largest city in Canada. If you went there, you could see one of the world's tallest structures, the CN Tower, soaring above the skyline. Montreal is one of Canada's oldest cities and has many historical buildings. It also has an important seaport, even though it is nearly 1,500 kilometres from the Atlantic Ocean!

Canada's official languages are English and French. But many other languages are spoken there, including Inukitut (the language of the Inuit, or Eskimos) and other Canadian Indian languages. Canadian Indians are also known as First Nations people.

If you visit Canada, you should try to see Niagara Falls. These beautiful waterfalls, on the border between Canada and the United States, were once one of the most famous honeymoon spots in North America.

Ottawa

SEARCH LIGHT

What is the only country larger than Canada?

LEARN MORE! READ THESE ARTICLES...
AN INUIT TALE: HOW CROW BROUGHT DAYLIGHT
TO THE WORLD (VOLUME 5)
OTTAWA, CANADA (VOLUME 9) • WHEAT (VOLUME 10)

Banff National Park in Alberta is one of Canada's major tourist destinations.
© David Muench/Corbis

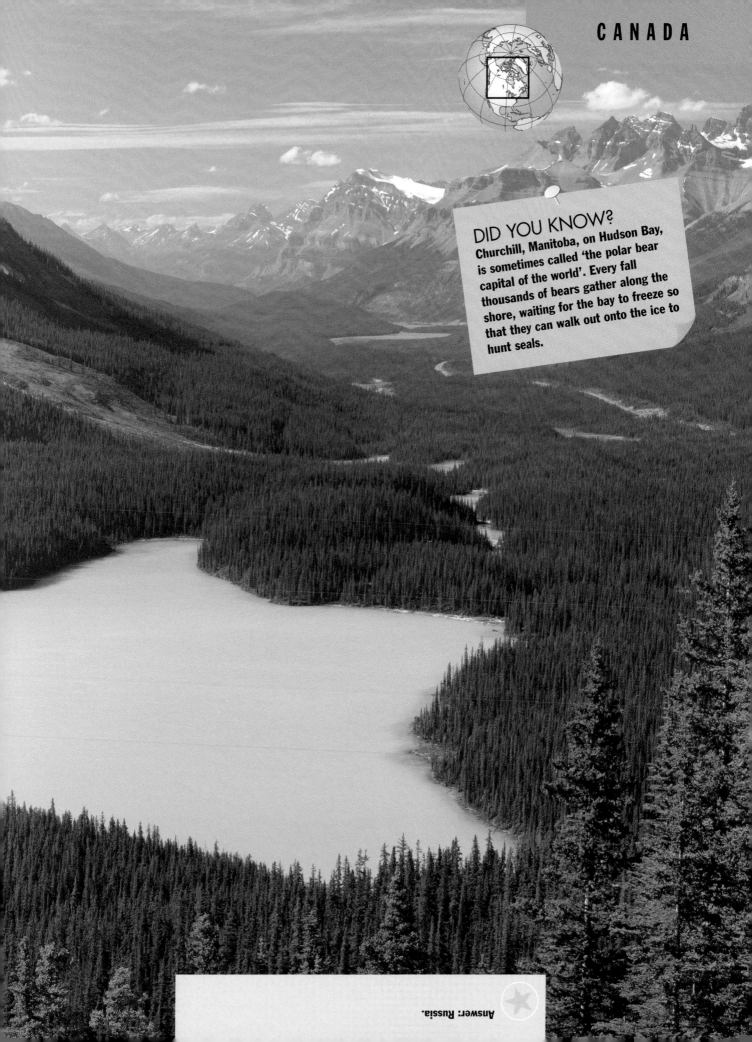

DID YOU KNOW?
Churchill, Manitoba, on Hudson Bay, is sometimes called 'the polar bear capital of the world'. Every fall thousands of bears gather along the shore, waiting for the bay to freeze so that they can walk out onto the ice to hunt seals.

Answer: Russia.

A Frozen Little Town

SEARCH LIGHT

The little town of Aklavik is in the Inuvik region, in the Northwest Territories of Canada. It's not far from the place where the Mackenzie River flows into the Arctic Ocean. In the Inuit (or Eskimo) language, *aklavik* means a place 'where there are bears'.

It is very cold there. The land is mostly frozen. It's above the Arctic Circle, which means that there are winter days when the Sun never rises - and summer days when it never

If it stays dark so much of the time and it's very cold, why would people have moved to Aklavik in the first place? (Hint: There's a clue in the name's meaning.)

sets. The people who live there are mostly Inuits and First Nations people (the name many Canadian Indians prefer to be called).

A long time ago the people around Aklavik hunted seals with spears called 'harpoons'. They also hunted bears and other animals with bows and arrows. They fished from small boats called 'kayaks'. To travel over land during the long winter, they used sledges drawn by dogs. Today

Children playing ice hockey in the street, Inuvik, Northwest Territories.
© Lowell Georgia/Corbis

the people of Aklavik still hunt, trap, and fish, but they get around in snowmobiles. The town now also has modern businesses, a radio station, and a weather office.

Aklavik was first set up as a fur-trading post in 1912. Fur garments and Inuit crafts were made there. But by the 1950s flooding and **erosion** had made it difficult to build houses, roads, and sewers in Aklavik. The Canadian government began building a new town called Inuvik about 53 kilometres away. Many people from Aklavik moved to Inuvik. But others insisted on staying, and the town's motto became 'Never say die'. In 2001 there were only 632 people left living in this little town.

LEARN MORE! READ THESE ARTICLES…
CANADA (VOLUME 9) • FLOODS (VOLUME 1)
AN INUIT TALE: HOW CROW BROUGHT DAYLIGHT TO THE WORLD (VOLUME 5)

A cold winter comes to the little town of Aklavik, in the Inuvik region of the Northwest Territories. Here you can see the Mackenzie River and the frozen land surrounding the town, as seen from above.
© Lowell Georgia/Corbis

Answer: Aklavik means 'where there are bears'. The early Inuits were hunters and lived by following bears and seals.

A Welcoming Northern Capital

SEARCH LIGHT

Find and correct the mistake in the following sentence: French and Canadian are the official languages of Canada.

Ottawa, the capital of Canada, is one of the country's most attractive cities. It is located on the south side of the Ottawa River in the province of Ontario. Across the river is the province of Quebec.

Since Ottawa is the centre of the country's government, it is the public face of Canada for many people. The city has been kept lovely and welcoming. It has many parks and rivers, bicycle paths, museums, art galleries, and universities. Some of Ottawa's historic buildings go back to the early 1800s. The Château Laurier is one of these. It is a house built in the style of a grand French **château**. Behind it rises Major's Hill Park, Ottawa's oldest park. This is the best place to view the city and to see up and down the Ottawa River.

Château Laurier, Ottawa, Ontario.
© Richard T. Nowitz/Corbis

Dozens of different languages are spoken in Ottawa. But most people speak either French or English, the official languages of Canada.

Many years ago French explorers and hunters travelled through the area that is now Ottawa. Only a few people lived there until the early 1800s. By that time the British ruled the territory. They decided they wanted a route for their ships to be able to travel from the Ottawa River to Lake Ontario, so they built the Rideau Canal. The city of Ottawa began as a base for the workers who built the **canal**. It was called Bytown then but later became Ottawa. It became the capital of Canada in the mid-1800s.

LEARN MORE! READ THESE ARTICLES...
CANADA (VOLUME 9) • ENGLAND (VOLUME 6) • FRANCE (VOLUME 6)

The Rideau Canal in Ottawa is the world's longest outdoor ice-skating rink.
© Cheryl Conlon/Lonely Planet Images

DID YOU KNOW?

The city of Ottawa was named after an Indian group that once lived in the region. The Ottawa were known as great traders. The name Ottawa means 'to trade' or 'the at-home-anywhere people'.

Answer: French and English are the official languages of Canada.

DID YOU KNOW?
The Magdalen Islands in the Gulf of St Lawrence are one of Quebec's most popular vacation spots. People come to see the islands' many birds and mammals, especially the seals, who arrive every spring to have their young.

La Belle Province

Quebec is both the oldest and the largest in land area of Canada's ten provinces. It's the home of two attractive port cities and a countryside that is covered with forests, rivers, and lakes. No wonder it's known in French as La Belle Province, 'the beautiful province'.

Quebec City is the capital of Quebec province and the oldest city in Canada. It lies at the point where the St Lawrence and Saint-Charles rivers meet. The name Quebec comes from the Algonquian Indian word for 'where the river narrows'. About 240 kilometres southwest of Quebec City is Montreal, the largest city in the province. It's also Canada's second largest city.

Ice cream sign written in French and English, in Quebec City.
© Richard T. Nowitz/Corbis

The first European to visit the area was Jacques Cartier of France. In 1534 he landed at the site of a Huron Indian village. But it was another 70 years before the French settled in the area. In 1608 Samuel de Champlain founded the city of Quebec, establishing the first permanent **colony** in the region. It served as a fur-trading post for beaver, mink, and other pelts.

During the next 150 years, the French and British fought over Quebec and Montreal. Eventually, a treaty in 1763 granted the area to the British. During the American Revolution, the American colonists tried to seize control of the area. But the British held onto it.

Eight out of every ten people in Quebec are of French **ancestry**. Because of this, both French and English are spoken in Quebec. The people of the province also practice different religions. Generally, the people of French origins are Roman Catholic and those of English origins are Protestant.

SEARCH LIGHT

What does 'Quebec' mean?

LEARN MORE! READ THESE ARTICLES...
AMERICAN INDIANS (VOLUME 4)
CANADA (VOLUME 9) • FRANCE (VOLUME 6)

There are many beautiful buildings in the Old Quebec historic area of Quebec City. The historic hotel Château Frontenac towers over the area.
© Ron Watts/Corbis

Answer: It's an Algonquian Indian word for 'where the river narrows'.

The Capital Province

Ontario is the second largest of Canada's ten provinces in terms of land size. But with about 12 million people, it has the largest population by far. In fact, more than one-third of all Canadians live in Ontario. Almost all of them live in one of Ontario's many cities.

The largest city in the province, Toronto, is known for its cultural life. It is the headquarters of Canada's national radio and television broadcasting. The city also has orchestras, choirs, national opera and ballet companies, and many art galleries and museums.

Ontario's other cities have their attractions as well. Ottawa is Canada's capital and is the home of the National Arts Centre. Stratford hosts the Stratford Festival, an annual theatre festival celebrating the plays of William Shakespeare. Niagara-on-the-Lake is the site of a theatre festival featuring the plays of George Bernard Shaw. And the natural beauty of Niagara Falls draws people to Ontario from all over the world.

The CN Tower rises 555 metres, above the rest of the Toronto skyline. The communications tower is the world's tallest freestanding structure.
© Royalty-Free/Corbis

DID YOU KNOW?
Ontario has more immigrants than any other province of Canada. The city of Toronto and its suburbs, in particular, are home to more than one-third of all the people who moved to Canada from another country.

The name Ontario comes from the word that the Iroquois Indian nation used for Lake Ontario. It may mean either 'sparkling water' or 'rocks standing by the water', referring to Niagara Falls. Lake Ontario is one of four Great Lakes that Ontario shares with the United States. The others are Superior, Huron, and Erie.

Tribes of the Iroquois and Algonquin nations were the first people in Ontario. Many Indians in Canada prefer to be called First Nations people. The first Europeans to meet them were French explorers. But Ontario was settled mainly by groups fleeing the American Revolution in the late 1700s and by people from the British Isles in the 1800s.

LEARN MORE! READ THESE ARTICLES...
AMERICAN INDIANS (VOLUME 4) · OTTAWA, CANADA (VOLUME 9)
THEATRE (VOLUME 3)

SEARCH LIGHT

True or false? The French were the first people to live in Ontario.

Answer: FALSE. Tribes of the Iroquois and Algonquin nations were the first people to live in the area.

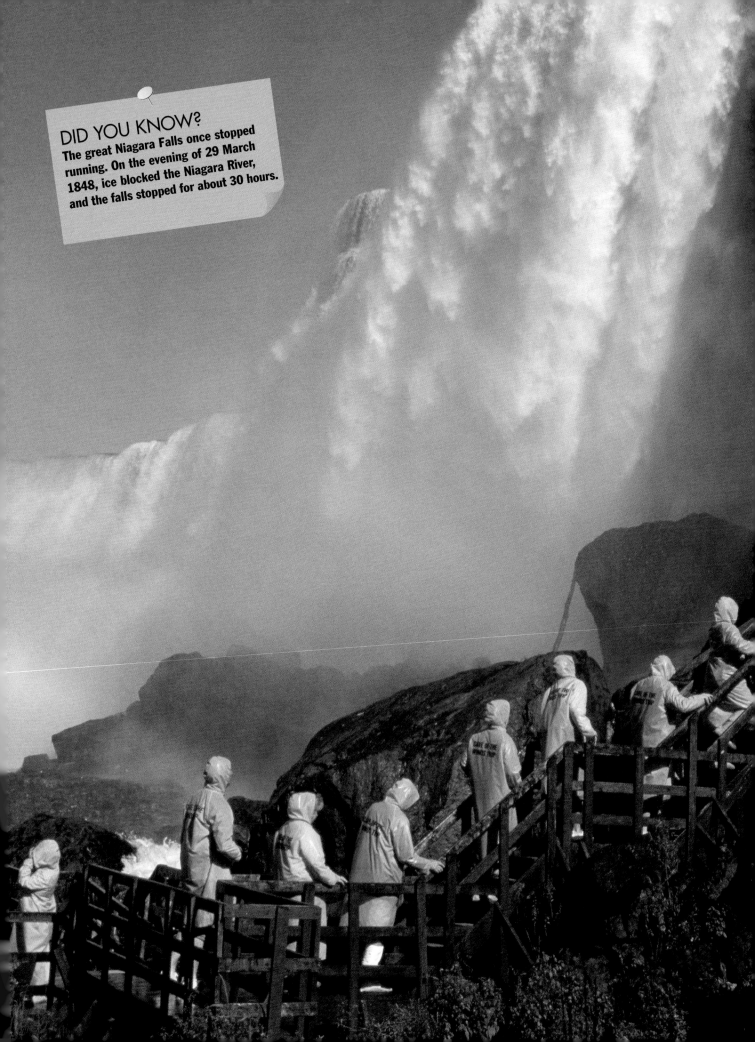

DID YOU KNOW?
The great Niagara Falls once stopped running. On the evening of 29 March 1848, ice blocked the Niagara River, and the falls stopped for about 30 hours.

Thunder of Waters

Niagara Falls, one of the most spectacular natural wonders in North America, is more than 25,000 years old. The falls are on the Niagara River, which flows between the United States and Canada, from Lake Erie to Lake Ontario.

Horseshoe Falls, the Canadian section of Niagara Falls.
© Dave G. Houser/Corbis

It is awesome just to be near the waterfall and watch the force of so many litres of water plunging down the steep cliff. More than 2.3 million litres per second pour over the falls. As the water thunders down, it fills the air with a silvery mist in which you can see many shining rainbows. A ceaseless roar fills the air as all this water strikes the bottom. The Iroquois Indians called this waterfall Niagara, meaning 'thunder of waters'.

The falls are divided into two parts by Goat Island. The larger portion is the Canadian section, known as the Horseshoe Falls. It measures 790 metres along its curve and drops 49.4 metres. The American Falls are smaller and rockier. Their width is 305 metres across, and they drop about 51 metres.

Between the American Falls and Goat Island are the small Luna Island and the small Luna Falls, also called Bridal Veil Falls. There are caves behind the curtain of water of both these falls. One of these is the Cave of the Winds.

The best views of the falls are from Queen Victoria Park on the Canadian side, Prospect Point on the U.S. side, and Rainbow Bridge, which crosses between the two.

LEARN MORE! READ THESE ARTICLES…
ONTARIO (VOLUME 9) • RIVERS (VOLUME 9)
VICTORIA FALLS (VOLUME 8)

SEARCH LIGHT

Find and correct the error in the following sentence: Niagara Falls is more than 2,500 years old.

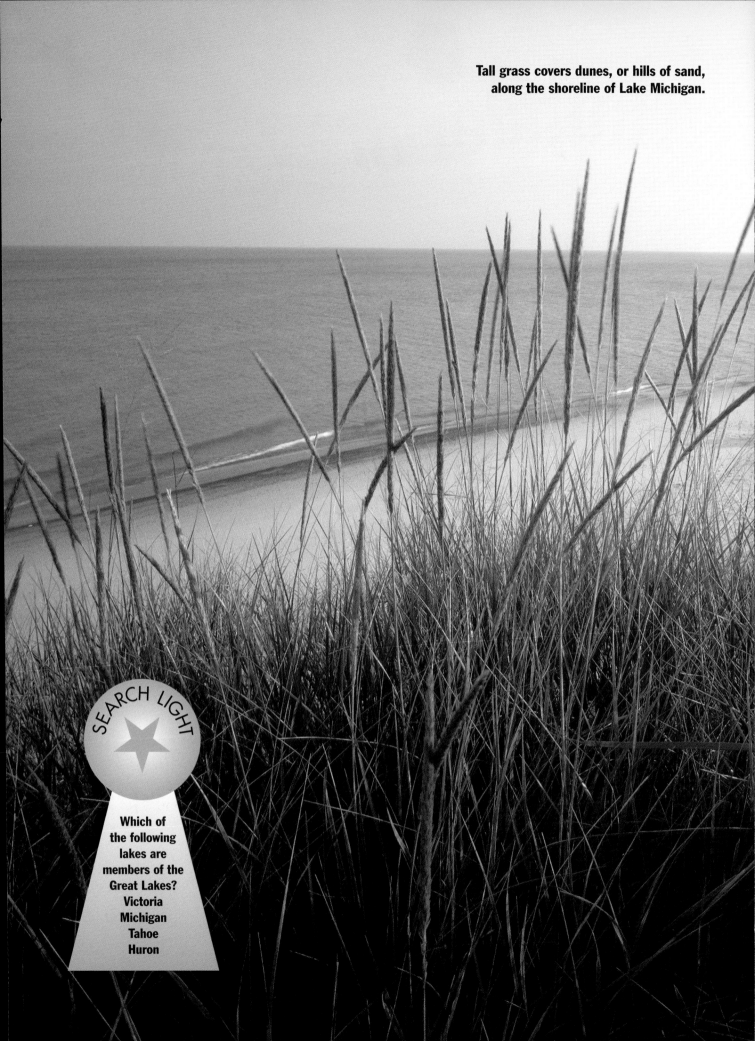

Tall grass covers dunes, or hills of sand, along the shoreline of Lake Michigan.

SEARCH LIGHT

Which of the following lakes are members of the Great Lakes?
Victoria
Michigan
Tahoe
Huron

America's Glacier Leftovers

The Great Lakes are a group of natural freshwater lakes in the middle of North America. These five lakes are Lake Superior, Lake Michigan, Lake Huron, Lake Erie, and Lake Ontario. The total area of the five lakes is larger than that of many countries, such as the United Kingdom.

The lakes were originally formed when **glaciers** retreated during the last Ice Age. The glaciers, giant chunks of ice, dug out the lake beds as they slowly moved. When the glaciers melted, their water filled the lakes.

Four of the five lakes act as a natural border between Canada and the United States. The fifth, Lake Michigan, is totally within the United States. Each one of the five lakes is special in some way. Lake Superior is the biggest as well as the deepest of the lakes. Lake Ontario is the smallest lake. Lake Erie is the shallowest lake. Lake Huron has the longest shoreline.

(Top) Boats in Lake Michigan at the start of a race from Chicago to Mackinac Island, Michigan; (bottom) Split Rock Lighthouse overlooking the waters of Lake Superior.

The water in the Great Lakes comes from many sources. Apart from rainfall, many streams, brooks, and small rivers empty into the lakes. Also, water from a lake at a higher **elevation** can overflow and drain into these lakes. And underground water seeps into the lakes from the surrounding land.

People enjoy visiting the lakes for fun activities such as swimming, motor boating, and sailing. Sandy beaches and parks alongside the lakes provide picnicking and camping areas. But because of **pollution**, the water of the lakes had once become very dirty. This was harming the fish in the lakes and nearby wildlife. Many groups concerned about the pollution are now busy trying to keep the waters clean.

LEARN MORE! READ THESE ARTICLES...
GLACIERS (VOLUME 1) • NIAGARA FALLS (VOLUME 9)
NORTH AMERICA (VOLUME 9)

DID YOU KNOW?

There are more than 30,000 islands in Lake Huron, including Manitoulin Island, the largest freshwater island in the world.

Answer: Michigan and Huron are two of the Great Lakes.

© AP/Wide World Photos

© Joseph Sohm/Corbis

© David Muench/Corbis

A Wealth of Resources and Beauty

The United States of America is rich in resources and natural beauty. This large country in North America is made up of 50 states, including Alaska and the islands of Hawaii in the Pacific Ocean. Its capital is Washington, D.C.

The United States is a **vast** and varied country, with forests, deserts, prairies, volcanoes, and **polar regions**. The country's mountain ranges include the Rocky Mountains and Sierra Nevadas in the west and the Appalachian Mountains in the east. The country's highest peak is Mount McKinley in Alaska. Native Americans call this mountain Denali, meaning 'The High One'. The United States has a number of mighty rivers, including the Colorado, the Columbia, and the Mississippi. The Mississippi

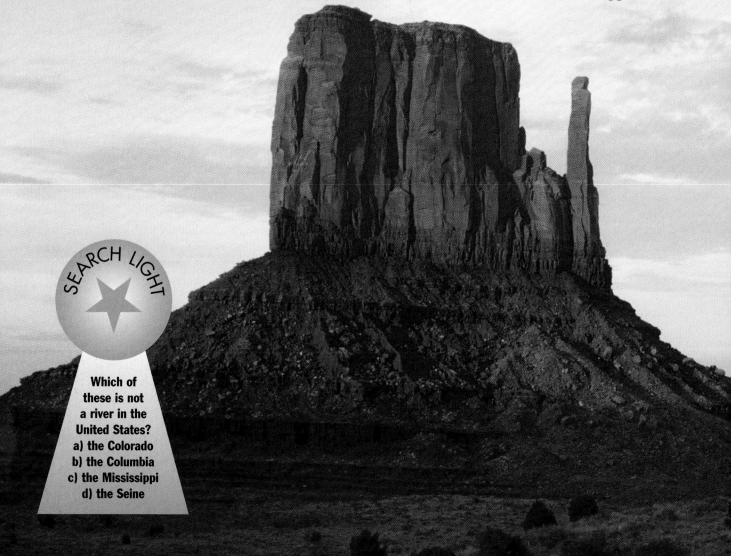

SEARCH LIGHT

Which of these is not a river in the United States?
a) the Colorado
b) the Columbia
c) the Mississippi
d) the Seine

River was the setting for many famous stories by the writer Mark Twain. The largest lakes are the five Great Lakes and the Great Salt Lake.

The country's farmlands produce maize, soybeans, wheat, and other crops that are sold to countries all over the world. With a wealth of forests, the United States is one of the world's leading producers of **timber**. It is also among the leading fishing nations, and it produces large amounts of copper, silver, gold, coal, **petroleum**, and natural gas. This **abundance** helped to make it the richest nation in the world.

The United States is also graced with features of great beauty. The major **scenic** attractions include the Grand Canyon in Arizona, Carlsbad Caverns in New Mexico, and Niagara Falls in New York state.

LEARN MORE! READ THESE ARTICLES...
GRAND CANYON (VOLUME 9) • MARK TWAIN (VOLUME 4)
UNITED STATES: A YOUNG AND POWERFUL NATION (VOLUME 9)

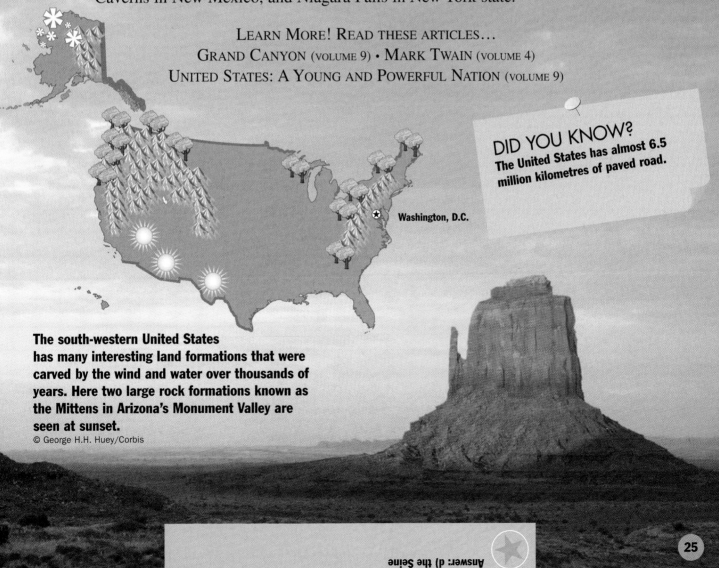

Washington, D.C.

DID YOU KNOW?
The United States has almost 6.5 million kilometres of paved road.

The south-western United States has many interesting land formations that were carved by the wind and water over thousands of years. Here two large rock formations known as the Mittens in Arizona's Monument Valley are seen at sunset.
© George H.H. Huey/Corbis

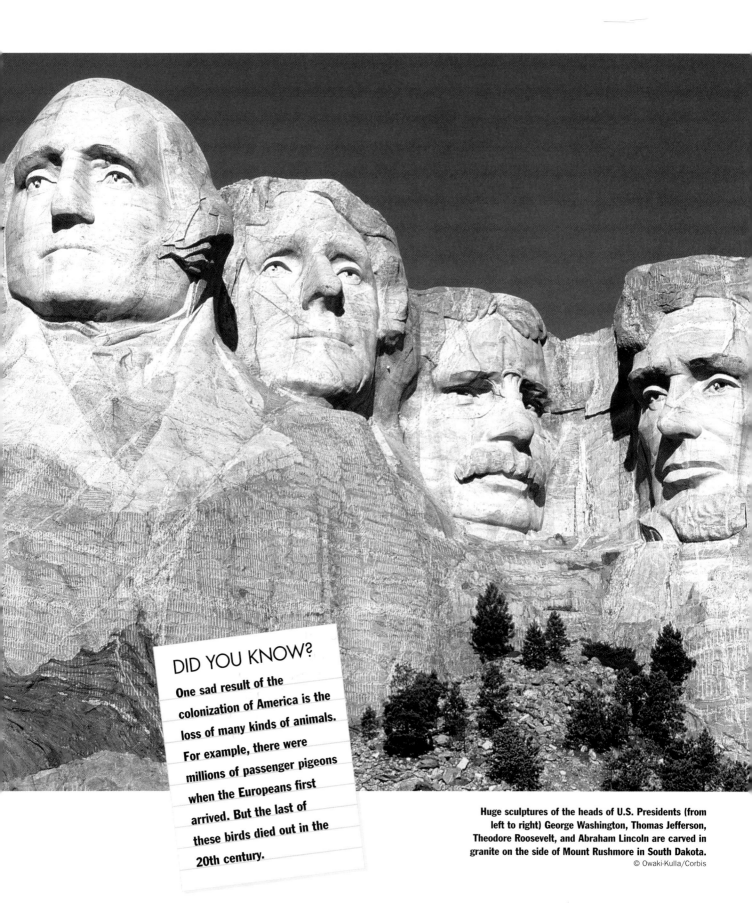

DID YOU KNOW?

One sad result of the colonization of America is the loss of many kinds of animals. For example, there were millions of passenger pigeons when the Europeans first arrived. But the last of these birds died out in the 20th century.

Huge sculptures of the heads of U.S. Presidents (from left to right) George Washington, Thomas Jefferson, Theodore Roosevelt, and Abraham Lincoln are carved in granite on the side of Mount Rushmore in South Dakota.

© Owaki-Kulla/Corbis

A Young and Powerful Nation

The history of the Americas changed forever in 1492 when Christopher Columbus sailed there from Spain. Shortly after his voyage, many other sailors arrived from Europe. These explorers and settlers took over the land that would become the United States. But they were not the first people

Missouri's famed Gateway Arch in St. Louis.
© Kelly-Mooney Photography/Corbis

there. The Europeans took the land from the more than 200 different groups of Native Americans, or Indians, who were living there.

The Spanish were among the first Europeans to build **colonies** there. Later the French and the British established colonies of their own. The first lasting British settlement in North America was founded in 1607 in Jamestown, in what was later the state of Virginia. It was quickly followed by other settlements all along the Atlantic coastline. Soon there were 13 colonies. They remained under British rule until 1776, when the colonists began a war for independence, called the American Revolutionary War.

Total freedom from the British came in 1783. A new **constitution** was created. George Washington, the leader of the Continental Army, became the first president of the United States of America. Within several years the city of Washington, in the District of Columbia, had been built to be the new nation's capital.

Over the next century and a half, the United States spread westward, gaining new territory, until it reached the Pacific Ocean. In the mid-20th century, two more states joined the rest of the United States. The island state of Hawaii, in the central Pacific, and the state of Alaska, which borders north-western Canada, brought the total to 50 states. Millions of immigrants from around the world have moved to the country. It has offered many the opportunity for a more comfortable and healthier life.

SEARCH LIGHT

True or false?
The land that is now the United States has always been ruled by U.S. citizens.

LEARN MORE! READ THESE ARTICLES...
AMERICAN INDIANS (VOLUME 4)
UNITED STATES: MELTING POT OF MANY CULTURES (VOLUME 9)
WASHINGTON, D.C., U.S. (VOLUME 9)

Answer: FALSE. American Indian groups lived on the land first. Then Europeans took over various areas. The United States did not become an independent country until the 1700s.

Melting Pot of Many Cultures

Dear Class,

We are in Boston, on the north-eastern coast of the United States, visiting my brother Rex after a few busy days of sightseeing. We've already been to New York City and Niagara Falls. Later we're going to take a look at the Grand Canyon, Hollywood, and Disneyland. Rex teaches history in one of the universities here. He's invited some of his friends to meet us.

Italian immigrants arriving at New York's Ellis Island.
© Bettmann/Corbis

One of them is from Austria, and another is from Poland. The rest are from Japan, India, and Italy. I tell him that I'm confused. 'Don't you have any American friends?' I ask Rex.

He laughs. 'They're all Americans.'

Helmut, his friend from Austria, says, 'Didn't you know that America has people from all over the world?'

'That's why people often describe America as a "melting pot" of many cultures,' says Tajima, from Japan.

'People come here for many reasons. Some become citizens. But students from all over the world also come here to study. I have students from Indonesia, Australia, Iran, and even Iceland in my college,' says Rex.

'But who were the first to come here?'

Rex's Indian friend, Samir, says the first people who came here were from Asia, more than 20,000 years ago. The American Indians (Native Americans) are their **descendants**. About 500 years ago, Spanish settlers arrived from Europe. Other Europeans followed - from England, Ireland, and Germany and then from Italy, Poland, Russia, Sweden, Greece, and elsewhere. People from Africa were first brought over as slaves. People from every corner of the world have made America what it is today.

Tonight we're going out for a Lebanese meal. I can't wait!
Your classmate,
Lydia

LEARN MORE! READ THESE ARTICLES...
ASIA (VOLUME 7) • EUROPE (VOLUME 6)
UNITED STATES: A YOUNG AND POWERFUL NATION (VOLUME 9)

SEARCH LIGHT

Fill in the gap with the correct phrase: When people call America a 'melting pot', they mean people from _____ live there.

New U.S. citizens recite the Pledge of Allegiance during a ceremony held in Miami, Florida's Orange Bowl Stadium.
© Bettmann/Corbis

DID YOU KNOW?

Christopher Columbus often gets credit as having been the first European in the Americas. But many researchers believe he was about 500 years too late. They think Leif Ericson, the Viking explorer, landed in North America first.

Answer: When people call America a 'melting pot', they mean people from all over the world live there.

29

Find and correct the mistake in the following sentence: The Capitol is the home and office of the president of the United States.

A view of Washington, D.C., from above shows (from front to rear) the Lincoln Memorial, the Washington Monument, and the Capitol.

Capital City of the U.S.A.

Washington, D.C., is the capital of the United States of America. The 'D.C.' stands for District of Columbia. President George Washington chose the site for the capital city, and the city was built especially as a home for the government.

Pierre-Charles L'Enfant, an **engineer** and artist, designed the city layout. The main roads of Washington, D.C., **extend** from the city centre like the rays of the Sun. These avenues are named after some of the states of the United States.

Tourists in paddleboats enjoy views of the Jefferson Memorial.
© Richard T. Nowitz/Corbis

Today Washington, D.C., has many monuments, museums, and official buildings that are connected with the government and the history of the United States. Most of these are grouped together in and around a large park-like area called the Mall.

Both the Washington Monument and the Lincoln Memorial are part of the Mall. The Lincoln Memorial, built to honour President Abraham Lincoln, is at one end of the Mall on the bank of the Potomac River. The Washington Monument, built to honour President Washington, is a huge granite obelisk, or **tapered** stone pillar. This monument is among the world's tallest stone structures. A memorial to President Thomas Jefferson is located south of the Mall. Two other memorials on the Mall honour the Americans who died in the Korean and Vietnam wars.

The White House is the office and home of the president of the United States. The Capitol is the building where the U.S. **Congress** meets and laws are made. It is one of the best-known landmarks in the United States. The **Supreme Court** and the Library of Congress are both close to the Capitol. The Library of Congress has the largest collection of books, maps, newspapers, documents, and **manuscripts** in the world.

DID YOU KNOW?
The Library of Congress in Washington, D.C., has more than 800 kilometres of shelves to hold everything it owns. But don't ask how many books are on those shelves. No one is really sure.

LEARN MORE! READ THESE ARTICLES...
ARCHITECTURE (VOLUME 3) • LONDON, ENGLAND (VOLUME 6)
UNITED STATES: A YOUNG AND POWERFUL NATION (VOLUME 9)

Answer: The White House is the home and office of the president of the United States.

Nature's Masterpiece

A canyon is a deep steep-walled valley cut through rock by a river. The word 'canyon' comes from the Spanish word *cañón*, which means 'tube'. Such valleys are found where river currents are strong and swift. A smaller valley cut out in the same way is called a 'gorge'.

Rafting through the Grand Canyon on the Colorado River.
© Kevin Fleming/Corbis

The Grand Canyon, in northern Arizona state in the United States, is the most beautiful and awesome canyon in the world. It is cut about a kilometre and a half deep into the earth and is known for its fantastic shapes and colours. Swiftly flowing water, sand, gravel, and mud gave the rocks their interesting shapes. Each of its rock layers has a different shade of colour, including **buff**, grey, green, pink, brown, and violet.

The canyon is 446 kilometres long and has been carved through the Arizona landscape by the Colorado River. It stretches in a zigzag course from the northern end of Arizona to the Grand Wash Cliffs near Nevada.

Many ancient pueblos - Native American cliffside dwellings - and other ruins in the canyon show that prehistoric peoples lived there. The Grand Canyon was first discovered by Europeans in 1540. It was established as a national park in 1919.

Visitors to the park can take a mule-pack trip down to the bottom of the canyon. People can even go river rafting, taking a thrilling trip over the rapids.

If you visit the canyon, you'll probably see some of the many animals that live there. Squirrels, coyotes, foxes, deer, badgers, bobcats, rabbits, chipmunks, and kangaroo rats all make their homes near the canyon.

In 1979 the Grand Canyon was named a World Heritage site.

LEARN MORE! READ THESE ARTICLES...
AMERICAN INDIANS (VOLUME 4) • PAUL BUNYAN (VOLUME 5)
RIVERS (VOLUME 1)

SEARCH LIGHT

Fill in the gap: The word 'canyon' comes from the Spanish word for '_____'.

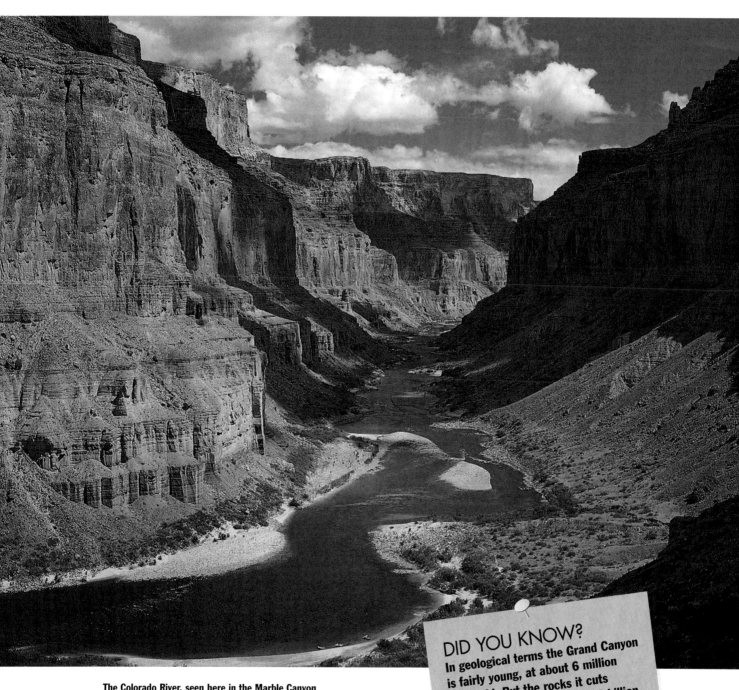

The Colorado River, seen here in the Marble Canyon
portion of the Grand Canyon, cut the whole canyon -
over millions of years.
Gary Ladd

DID YOU KNOW?
In geological terms the Grand Canyon
is fairly young, at about 6 million
years old. But the rocks it cuts
through date back as far as 2 billion
to 2.5 billion years ago.

Answer: The word 'canyon' comes from the Spanish word for 'tube'.

33

Waikiki Beach, with Diamond Head in the background, is the centre for tourism in Honolulu. There are many big resorts along the beach, and people come from all over the world to enjoy swimming and surfing in the waters of the Pacific Ocean.

SEARCH LIGHT

Diamond Head is a
a) sunken battleship.
b) rare gem.
c) crater of a volcano.

Crossroads
of the Pacific

It is said that no place on Earth has better weather than Honolulu. In the course of an entire year, the temperature rarely gets below 14°C or above 31°C. And the sun is usually shining. Honolulu is the capital of Hawaii, a state made up of islands in the middle of the Pacific Ocean. Hawaii became the 50th American state in 1959.

Iolani Palace, Honolulu, Hawaii.
© Michael T. Sedam/Corbis

Honolulu is on Oahu Island. Like Hawaii's other large islands, Oahu formed from material that spewed up from volcanoes on the ocean floor. Diamond Head, the crater, or centre, of an old volcano, is one of the best-known landmarks in the Pacific. It got the name Diamond Head when some British sailors found crystals on its slopes and mistakenly thought they were diamonds!

Polynesian people from other Pacific islands were probably the first settlers in Honolulu, but Europeans did not arrive until 1794. That is when Captain William Brown of the British ship *Butterworth* entered the harbour.

Today the modern city of Honolulu is a major port. In the Hawaiian language, its name means 'protected bay'. It is also called 'the crossroads of the Pacific' because of the many ships and airplanes that stop there.

Sun, sand, and sea attract many tourists to Waikiki Beach. Most visitors also go to see the USS *Arizona*, a sunken battleship. It was left in place as a memorial to all the people who died in Japan's attack on Pearl Harbor on 7 December 1941. This attack is what brought the United States into World War II.

DID YOU KNOW?
There are only 12 letters in the Hawaiian alphabet. A, E, I, O, and U are the vowels, and H, K, L, M, N, P, and W are the consonants.

LEARN MORE! READ THESE ARTICLES...
ISLANDS (VOLUME 1)
UNITED STATES: A WEALTH OF RESOURCES AND BEAUTY (VOLUME 9)
VOLCANOES (VOLUME 1)

Answer: c) crater of a volcano.

There are many things to do in New York City's Central Park. The park has a zoo, an ice-skating rink, an open-air theatre, a band shell, athletic playing fields and children's playgrounds, and paths for biking and walking.
© David Ball/Corbis

SEARCH LIGHT

Which of these sights can be found in New York City?
a) the Statue of Liberty
b) the White House
c) Central Park
d) the Empire State Building
e) the Sears Tower

City of Liberty

New York City has the largest population of any city in the United States. Located where the Hudson and East rivers join New York Bay, it is also an important port. The city is made up of five parts called boroughs: Manhattan, Brooklyn, the Bronx, Queens, and Staten Island. People from all over the world have moved to New York City to live and work there. It's known for its famous museums, towering skyscrapers, and jostling crowds.

New York has many well-known landmarks. The famous Statue of Liberty rises up from the harbour. It has become a symbol of the city. Other well-known sights are the Brooklyn Bridge, Times Square, and the

Close-up view of the arm and torch of the Statue of Liberty.
© Ron Watts/Corbis

fun fair at Coney Island. The city also houses the headquarters of the international organization known as the United Nations.

New York is one of the most popular tourist cities in the world, but it suffered a disaster in 2001 that caused some people to stay away for awhile. On 11 September, **terrorists** flew two planes into the twin towers of the World Trade Center, which were the city's tallest buildings. Thousands of people died when both towers collapsed. But the city's spirit helped it make a strong recovery.

Today the Empire State Building is the tallest building in New York City. From the top you can look down and see the whole city spread out below. The large patch of green that you see from the Empire State Building is Central Park. Even though it is in the middle of a big city, it is one of the best bird-watching places along the whole East Coast of the United States.

LEARN MORE! READ THESE ARTICLES…
NEW YORK CITY, U.S.: THE GREAT CULTURE MART (VOLUME 9)
PARIS, FRANCE (VOLUME 6)
UNITED STATES OF AMERICA: A YOUNG AND POWERFUL NATION (VOLUME 9)

Answer: The Statue of Liberty, the Empire State Building, and Central Park are all famous tourist spots in New York City.

The Great Culture Mart

Many people describe New York City as the centre of culture in the United States. That's because no matter what you're interested in, you'll find it in New York. Whether it's theatre, music, ballet, or museums, the city has some of the very best to offer.

The street called Broadway in New York became the centre of American theatre in the mid-19th century. The number, size, and

Fill in the gaps: Carnegie Hall is a famous _____ _____ in New York City.

fame of the Broadway theatres grew as New York City grew. In the 1890s the brilliantly lighted street became known as 'the Great White Way'. Beyond these theatres the city offers free performances of the plays of William Shakespeare in Central Park. Operas and concerts are also held in the park.

Dinosaur skeletons on exhibit at the American Museum of Natural History.
© Michael S. Yamashita/Corbis

New York City has a number of famous entertainment venues for performances of all kinds. The city's concert halls include those at the Lincoln Center for the Performing Arts as well as Carnegie Hall and Radio City Music Hall. The groups that perform in these halls include the Metropolitan Opera, the New York City Opera, and the New York **Philharmonic**. The New York City Ballet also performs at Lincoln Center, in the New York State Theater.

Museums are another important part of New York City's cultural life. The Metropolitan Museum of Art, the Museum of Modern Art, and the Guggenheim Museum are among the city's art museums. You can also spend many hours in the American Museum of Natural History and its Rose Center for Earth and Space Science. With all of these resources, there is always plenty to do in New York City.

LEARN MORE! READ THESE ARTICLES...
LONDON, ENGLAND (VOLUME 6)
NEW YORK CITY, U.S.: CITY OF LIBERTY (VOLUME 9) • THEATRE (VOLUME 3)

The Metropolitan Museum of Art is a favourite spot for visitors and New Yorkers alike. More than 5 million people visit the museum each year.
© Bob Krist/Corbis

DID YOU KNOW?
The Brooklyn Children's Museum was one of the world's first museums designed specifically for children. It was also one of the first to offer interactive activities for children.

Answer: Carnegie Hall is a famous concert hall in New York City.

Ring of Fire

Mexico is a large North American country with ancient cities, beautiful beaches, and snow-capped mountains. Many of the mountains are volcanoes. They are part of the 'Ring of Fire', a chain of volcanoes that form a circle around the Pacific Ocean.

The mountains are just one part of Mexico's diverse **geography**, which also includes deserts, grasslands, and tropical forests. The tropical forests, in southern Mexico, are home to such animals as monkeys, parrots, and jaguars. Deer, coyotes, snakes, and armadillos are found in the dry north.

Mexico's history goes back thousands of years. The native Indian Olmec were the first to establish a **civilization** in what is now Mexico. They lived in central Mexico from about 1200 to 400 BC. The Maya, Toltec, and Aztec later built their own cities. The Aztec city of Tenochtitlán was built on the site of what is now Mexico City, the country's capital.

In the 1500s Spanish conquistadores (soldiers) took over from the Aztec, and Spain ruled Mexico for several hundred years. The country gained its independence in the early 1900s. Because of this history, Mexican culture is part Indian and part Spanish. Although Spanish is the official language, there are about 50 other local languages spoken.

On 2 November, the *Dia de los Muertos* (Day of the Dead) is observed. Also called All Souls' Day, it is a time when families visit the graves of their dead ancestors. Another popular holiday is *Cinco de Mayo* (5 May), which celebrates a Mexican victory against an invading French army.

LEARN MORE! READ THESE ARTICLES...
MAYAN CIVILIZATION (VOLUME 4) • MEXICO CITY (VOLUME 9)
VOLCANOES (VOLUME 1)

Mexico City

The tower of the Great Palace and surrounding ruins are part of an ancient city in Mexico built by the Mayan people.
© ML Sinibaldi/Corbis

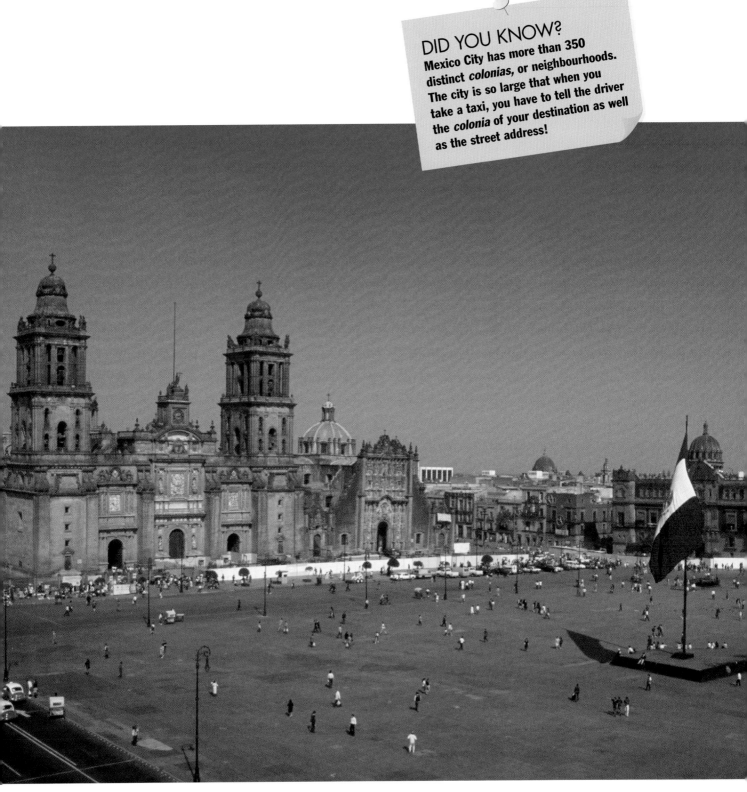

The centre of Mexico City is a square popularly known as the Zócalo.
The square is surrounded by many splendid public buildings.
© Randy Faris/Corbis

Sinking City of Palaces

Mexico City is the capital of Mexico and one of the world's largest cities, with more than 8 million people. It was founded in 1325 as the capital of the Aztec people. The Aztec city was called Tenochtitlán, which means 'Place of the High Priest Tenoch'.

The floating gardens of Xochimilco.
© Peter M. Wilson/Corbis

Tenochtitlán was built on small islands in Lake Texcoco. After Spanish conquerors arrived in the 16th century, they began draining the lake in order to use the land. Today most of the water is gone, but the soil is soft and some of the city's streets and buildings are sinking. Since 1900 the city has sunk about 9 metres!

Mexico City is high above sea level - about 2,240 metres. However, it is surrounded by mountain ranges that are much higher. Dust and smoke from cars, fires, and factories are trapped by the mountains and pollute the city's air. The city also lies within an earthquake zone. An earthquake in 1985 destroyed many buildings and killed thousands of people. But most of the city's ancient monuments and palaces remained unharmed.

Many of these monuments are located around a square called the Zócalo. They include the National Palace and the Metropolitan **Cathedral**. In another part of the city, Chapultepec Park includes a castle, a zoo, and a fun fair. The Pink Zone ('Zona Rosa') is one of Mexico City's main tourist and entertainment areas. It is the home of orchestras, art galleries, museums, theatre groups, and dance companies.

Another interesting area to visit is Xochimilco, with its floating gardens. These are rafts made out of reeds on which plants and flowers are grown. The famous Aztec pyramids of Teotihuacán are located north-east of the city.

SEARCH LIGHT

Mexico City was founded by
a) the Aztec.
b) the Inca.
c) the Maya.

LEARN MORE! READ THESE ARTICLES...
MEXICO (VOLUME 9) • MOUNTAINS (VOLUME 1) • PANAMA CITY, PANAMA (VOLUME 9)

Answer: a) the Aztec.

Blue poison dart frog.
© Kevin Schafer/Corbis

DID YOU KNOW?
No place in Central America is more than 200 kilometres from the sea. At its narrowest point, in Panama, the isthmus is only 48 kilometres across.

The ruins of the stone-stepped Temple of the Jaguar stand at the archaeological site at Tikal, Guatemala.
© John Noble/Corbis

Mayan painted tripod plate.
© Bowers Museum of Cultural Art/Corbis

The Isthmus Nations

Central America is an **isthmus** that lies between the Pacific Ocean and the Caribbean Sea. Seven countries lie within its boundaries - Belize, Guatemala, El Salvador, Honduras, Nicaragua, Costa Rica, and Panama. Together this cluster of nations stretches from North to South America. The countries share a long and proud history that reaches back thousands of years to the civilizations of the Maya and other native Indian peoples.

The Maya built great cities in northern Central America from about AD 200 to 900, but then they began to decline. When Spanish explorers arrived in the 16th century there were few Maya left. The Spanish soon established **colonies** in the area and ruled them for about 300 years before granting them independence. Because of this, most Central Americans speak Spanish, though many Indians speak their native languages. English is the official language of Belize, which was ruled by England for many years.

Today the people of the region are very diverse. Some are descended from Europeans, while others are of Asian or black African **ancestry** or Maya. Most are mestizos - people of mixed Indian and European ancestry.

Central America is mainly hilly and has many mountains. Swamps, rainforests, and lowlands extend along both coasts. There are many volcanoes, and the region has frequent earthquakes. Most people live along the western side.

Central America has many fascinating plants and animals, particularly in its rainforests. Jaguars and ocelots prowl the forest floors. Spider and howler monkeys scramble through the trees and climb vines called 'lianas'. Manatees swim in the rivers. Parrots chatter and insects buzz. Beautiful orchids bloom in clearings, and unusual fruits and nuts are found everywhere.

SEARCH LIGHT

Fill in the gap: Because of Central America's colonial past, most of its people speak _____.

LEARN MORE! READ THESE ARTICLES...
MAYAN CIVILIZATION (VOLUME 4)
NORTH AMERICA (VOLUME 9)
SOUTH AMERICA (VOLUME 9)

Land of the Quetzal

Guatemala is a country in Central America. It was once home to the great Mayan civilization, which ruled from about AD 250 to 900. Today Mayan Indians make up about half of Guatemala's population, and they still have a great influence on its culture. Their crafts, dances, music, and religious ceremonies are similar to those from hundreds of years ago.

Along with the Mayan Indians, the population of Guatemala includes the Ladinos, who have mixed Spanish and Mayan Indian heritage. While the Mayan Indians tend to live in the rural highlands, most Ladinos live in cities. The Ladinos tend to be wealthier than the Indians.

Spanish is the country's most widely spoken language, but one in three Guatemalans speaks an Indian language. Most of the people are Roman Catholic, but many Indians mix Catholic beliefs with traditional religious practices. The town of Esquipulas, in eastern Guatemala, is home to the Black Christ, the most important Catholic shrine in Central America. It was named for the dark wood from which it was carved. Guatemala's many religious festivals include the popular Easter celebrations in the town of Antigua Guatemala.

The land of Guatemala includes mountains, volcanoes, grasslands, and rainforests. The wildlife of the rainforests includes the quetzal, the colourful national bird. There are also many snakes, crocodiles, and iguanas.

Farming is important in Guatemala. Many farmers grow maize, beans, and squash to feed themselves and their families. Other farmers raise coffee, bananas, sugar-cane, cotton, and cattle to sell to other countries.

SEARCH LIGHT

Fill in the gap: Most people in Guatemala have at least some _____ ancestry.
a) French
b) Quetzal
c) Mayan Indian

LEARN MORE! READ THESE ARTICLES...
MAYAN CIVILIZATION (VOLUME 4) • MEXICO (VOLUME 9)
VOLCANOES (VOLUME 1)

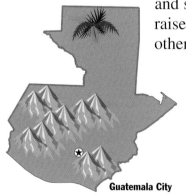

Guatemala City

For gorgeous feathers, few birds surpass the quetzal. Found in rainforests from southern Mexico to Bolivia, the quetzal was the sacred bird of the ancient Maya and Aztec. Today it is the national symbol of Guatemala (whose monetary unit is the quetzal).
© Michael & Patricia Fogden/Corbis

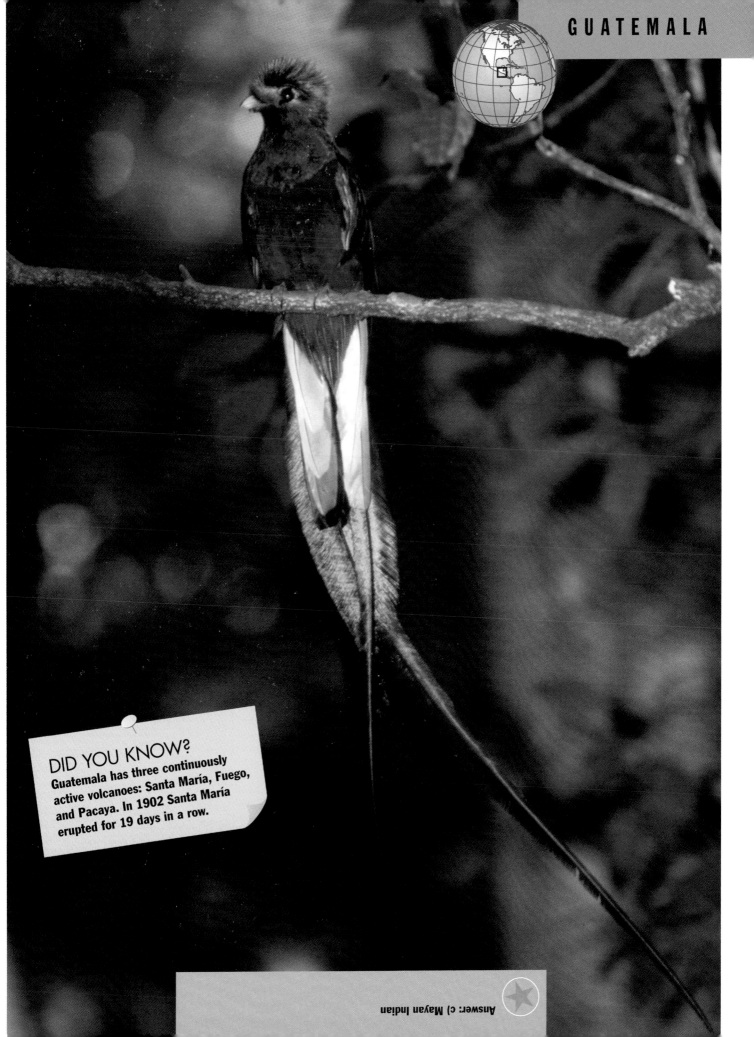

DID YOU KNOW?
Guatemala has three continuously active volcanoes: Santa María, Fuego, and Pacaya. In 1902 Santa María erupted for 19 days in a row.

Answer: c) Mayan Indian

SEARCH LIGHT

Why do you suppose Spanish is the official language of Nicaragua?

Ash clouds rise into the air during an eruption of Cerro Negro, Nicaragua's most active volcano.

Volcanoes and Earthquakes in Central America

Nicaragua is the largest country in Central America, the strip of land that connects North and South America. The capital and largest city of Nicaragua is Managua.

Nicaragua has two large lakes, Managua and Nicaragua. The area around the lakes is dotted with about 40 volcanoes. Some of the volcanoes are still active. Nicaragua also experiences many earthquakes, which can be very destructive.

Managua

The most **fertile** farmland in the country lies near the volcanoes. The soil is rich with **minerals** from volcanic ash. Because of that, people have lived in the area for thousands of years. The early people who lived there found this soil perfect for growing beans and maize. They were also skilled craftsmen and left behind stone carvings, pottery, and gold jewellery. But they also discovered the power of the volcanoes. Scientists have found footprints that were left many years ago by people who were fleeing from the lava and ash of an erupting volcano.

Spanish explorers arrived in Nicaragua in the 1500s. The native Indians who lived there resisted, but eventually the Spanish conquered the land. Nicaragua was named for Nicarao, an Indian chief who led the fight against the Spanish. The country finally gained independence from the Spanish in the 1800s.

Many Nicaraguans are farmers, still growing the traditional maize and beans. They also produce coffee, cotton, beef, and bananas, which are sold to other countries. Only a small portion of the land is actually used for farming, however. More than one-fourth of the country is covered with rainforest.

DID YOU KNOW?
Association football, or soccer, is the most popular sport in all Central American countries except for Nicaragua, where baseball is the national pastime.

LEARN MORE! READ THESE ARTICLES…
CENTRAL AMERICA (VOLUME 9) • RAINFORESTS (VOLUME 1)
VOLCANOES (VOLUME 1)

Answer: The Spanish conquered much of South and Central America in the 1500s and ruled the region for many centuries. For that reason Spanish is still the official language of Nicaragua, even though Spain no longer controls the country.

Land of
Many Fish

SEARCH LIGHT

What turned Panama City from a small fishing village into a centre for world trade?

Panama City is the capital of the small Central American country of Panama. It lies on the Gulf of Panama near the Panama **Canal**. Panama City used to be a small Indian fishing village. The Spanish name for the city, *Panamá*, means 'many fish'.

A Spanish soldier named Pedro Arias Dávila founded Panama City in 1519. It was the first European settlement on the Pacific coast of the Americas. After the Panama Canal opened in 1914, the city became an important centre for world trade.

To understand what the city looked like centuries ago, you can visit the area known as San Felipe. Some people call it Casco Viejo, which means 'old city'. Here you'll see many buildings from the **colonial** days. In the building called the Salón Bolívar, the soldier Simón Bolívar worked on ways to unify the South American countries newly freed from Spanish rule. In 1997 the United Nations Educational, Scientific and Cultural Organization named the old section of Panama City a World Heritage site. This means that it is an important cultural site that should be protected and preserved.

But it's the canal that connects the Atlantic Ocean with the Pacific Ocean that most visitors want to see. Every day ships from all over the world take the trip through the narrow canal. The ships carry **cargo** and passengers between countries. The canal saves them a journey of thousands of kilometres around the southern tip of South America.

LEARN MORE! READ THESE ARTICLES...
SIMÓN BOLÍVAR (VOLUME 4) • PANAMA CANAL (VOLUME 9)
TRANSPORTATION (VOLUME 2)

DID YOU KNOW?
Because of the way Panama curves, a very strange thing happens when you pass through the Panama Canal. Travelling through the canal from the Atlantic to the Pacific actually takes you from west to east instead of the other way around. So when you exit, even though you're on the west side of the country, you're farther east than when you started.

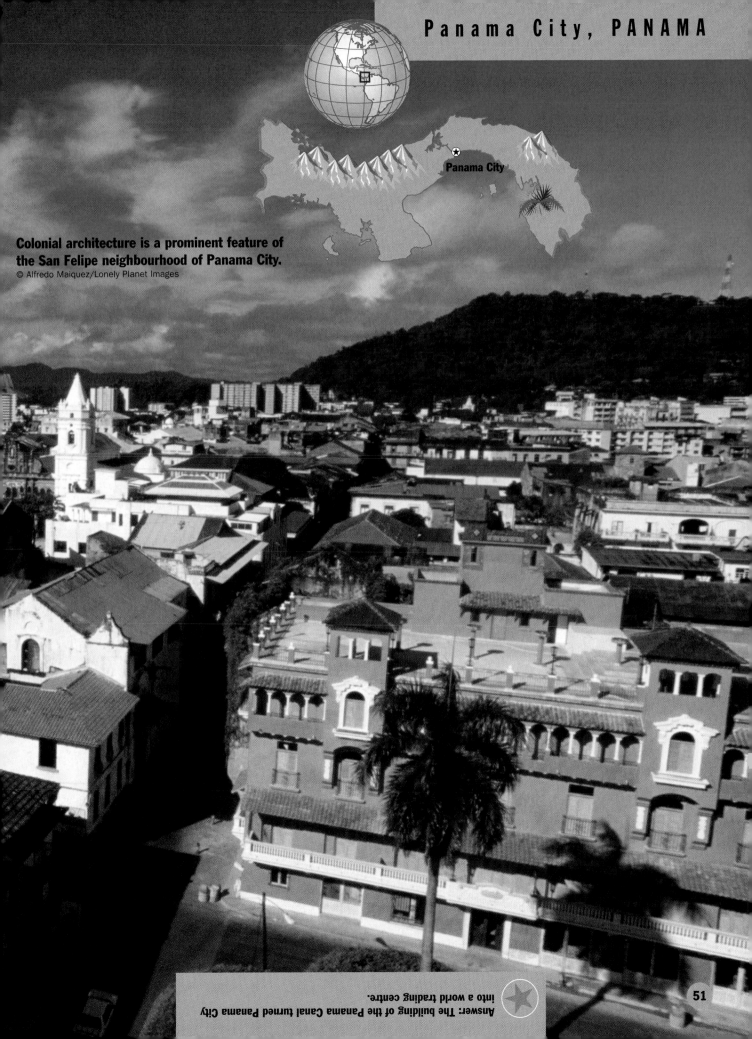

Panama City

Colonial architecture is a prominent feature of
the San Felipe neighbourhood of Panama City.
© Alfredo Maiquez/Lonely Planet Images

Answer: The building of the Panama Canal turned Panama City
into a world trading centre.

A Major World Waterway

The Panama Canal is one of the most important artificial waterways in the world. It's located in the Central American country of Panama. The canal cuts through a narrow strip of land to connect the Atlantic and Pacific oceans. It is about 80 kilometres long.

The Panama Canal can cut thousands of kilometres from a ship's voyage. Ships travelling between the east and west coasts of the United States, for example, can shorten their trip by more than 14,500 kilometres. Without the canal, they would have to go around the southern tip of South America.

Many different kinds of goods are shipped through the canal. Thousands of ships carry more than 180 million tonnes of **cargo** through it each year. The most important goods include **petroleum** and grains.

The Panama Canal uses what is called a lock system. Locks are huge tanks with gates at each end. They are used to raise or lower boats from one water level to another. This is necessary because the lake through which the canal passes is at a higher level than the oceans.

(Top) Construction of the Panama Canal; (bottom) two men stand in front of canal locks under construction in 1913 as part of the Panama Canal project.

First a boat enters the lock, and the gate is closed behind it. If the boat needs to rise to a higher level, water is added to the lock. As the water rises, the boat floats higher. When the lock is full of water, the gate in front of the boat is opened. The boat can then travel out onto the higher part of the canal. The process is reversed for boats going in the other direction. It takes about nine hours for a ship to go through the canal.

SEARCH LIGHT

How long does it take a ship to pass through the Panama Canal?

LEARN MORE! READ THESE ARTICLES...
PANAMA CITY, PANAMA (VOLUME 9) • SUEZ CANAL (VOLUME 8)
TRANSPORTATION (VOLUME 2)

A small tugboat leads a large ship out of one of the Panama Canal's locks.

DID YOU KNOW?

Boats pay to use the canal, just as cars do on some roads. A large cruise ship might pay more than £60,000. A man named Richard Halliburton paid the lowest toll ever recorded. He paid just about 22 pence when he swam the length of the canal in 1928.

Answer: The trip takes about nine hours.

Caribbean Paradise

In 1492, Christopher Columbus believed he had reached the Spice Islands in Asia by sailing west from Spain across the Atlantic Ocean. What he didn't know about were the other major islands and continents in between! Later, however, people realized that he had reached a land unknown to Europeans. They named the islands where he first landed the West Indies, to set them apart from the Spice Islands (the East Indies) of South-east Asia.

The West Indies are a long chain of islands that separate the Caribbean Sea from the Atlantic Ocean. They stretch for more than 3,200 kilometres between Florida in the United States and the northern coast of South America. Many islands have mountains, and some have active volcanoes. Sometimes, powerful and destructive **hurricanes** sweep across the West Indies.

After Columbus' visit, Spain and other European countries set up **colonies** in the West Indies. They also enslaved or killed the native Indians and brought slaves from Africa to work on rich sugarcane **plantations**. Slavery ended by the late 1800s. But the centuries of colonization, slavery, and other **immigration** led to the unique cultural blends of the various islands.

Many West Indian islands are independent countries. These include Cuba (the largest island), Jamaica, Grenada, Haiti, and Trinidad and Tobago. Other islands are controlled by or strongly tied to European countries or the United States. These islands and groups include Puerto Rico (United States), Bermuda (United Kingdom), and Aruba (Netherlands).

One thing many West Indian islands have in common, however, is their popularity with tourists. People enjoy their beautiful beaches, blue waters, and warm weather.

COUNTRIES AND TERRITORIES IN THE WEST INDIES
1. Antigua and Barbuda
2. Bahamas, The
3. Barbados
4. Cuba
5. Dominica
6. Dominican Republic
7. Grenada
8. Haiti
9. Jamaica
10. St. Kitts and Nevis
11. St. Lucia
12. St. Vincent and the Grenadines
13. Trinidad and Tobago

LEARN MORE! READ THESE ARTICLES...
CUBA (VOLUME 9) • SUGARCANE (VOLUME 10)
VOLCANOES (VOLUME 1)

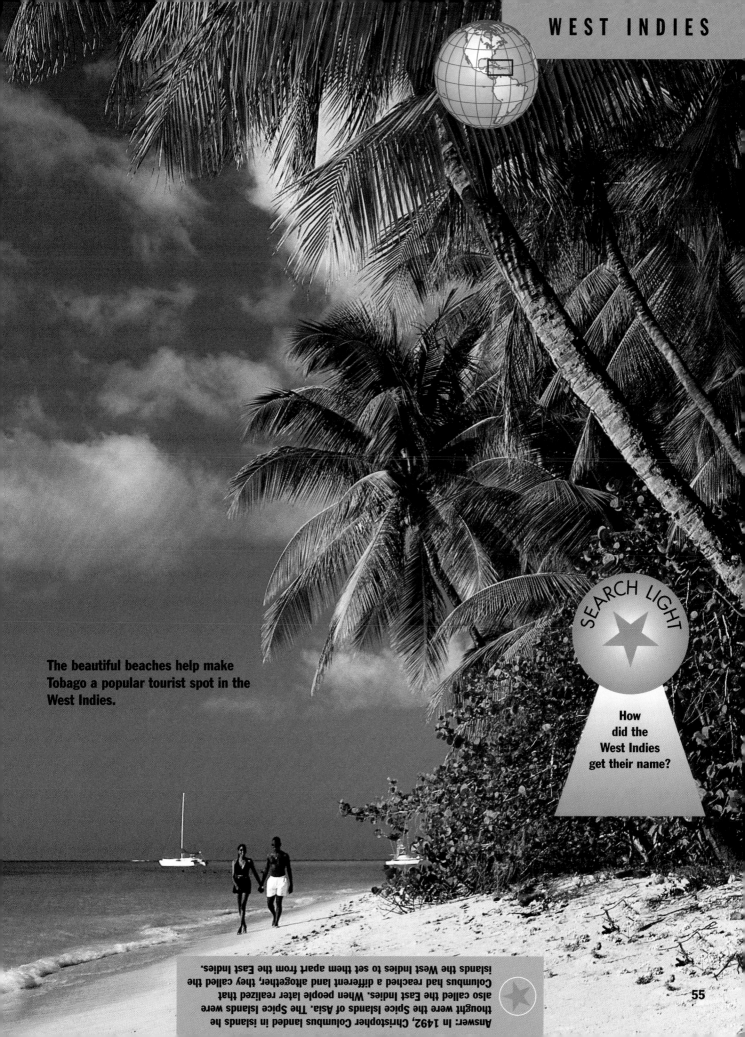

The beautiful beaches help make Tobago a popular tourist spot in the West Indies.

SEARCH LIGHT

How did the West Indies get their name?

Answer: In 1492, Christopher Columbus landed in islands he thought were the Spice Islands of Asia. The Spice Islands were also called the East Indies. When people later realized that Columbus had reached a different land altogether, they called the islands the West Indies to set them apart from the East Indies.

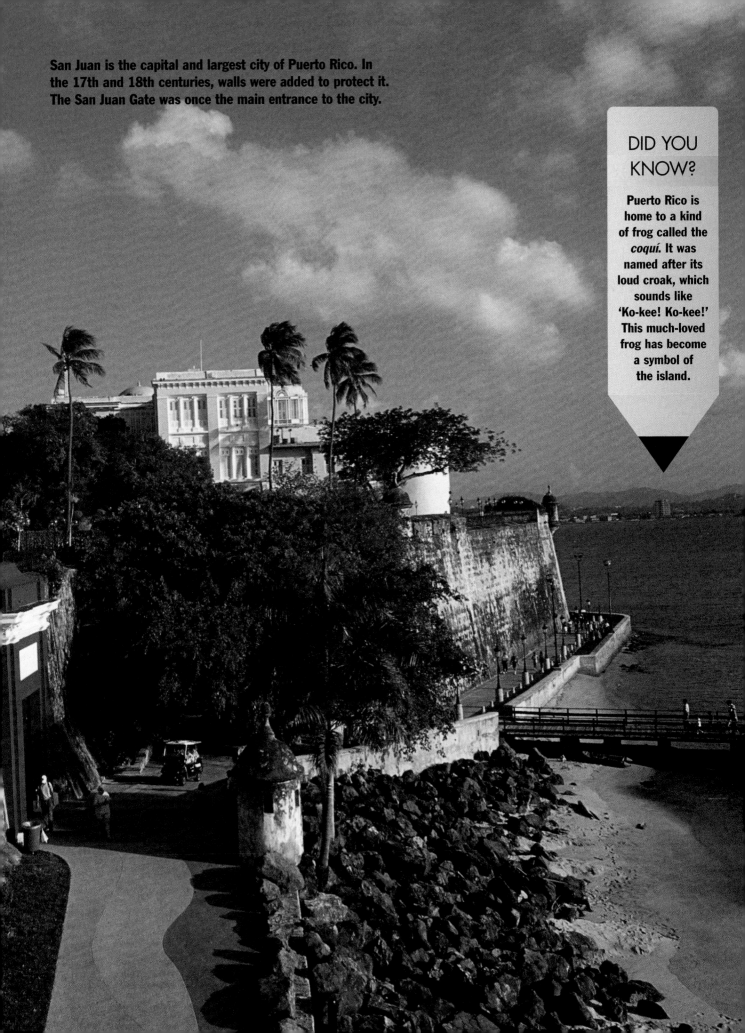

San Juan is the capital and largest city of Puerto Rico. In the 17th and 18th centuries, walls were added to protect it. The San Juan Gate was once the main entrance to the city.

DID YOU KNOW?

Puerto Rico is home to a kind of frog called the *coquí*. It was named after its loud croak, which sounds like 'Ko-kee! Ko-kee!' This much-loved frog has become a symbol of the island.

Jewel of the Caribbean

The island of Puerto Rico is a self-governing commonwealth of the United States. This means it has the right to make its own laws, but it has some ties with the United States. Puerto Ricans are American citizens, but they do not elect representatives to the U.S. Congress or pay U.S. taxes.

Located in the West Indies, Puerto Rico lies in the northern Caribbean Sea. The island is mostly hilly, though it is flatter along the coast. Most of the people live in the coastal area. Rainforests cover parts of the north. Many of the island's trees were cut down for lumber or farming. Special plans now encourage **conservation**. New forests have been planted with such fast-growing trees as eucalyptus, teak, and Honduran pine.

Puerto Rico was known as Borinquén to the native Arawak Indians who settled on the island hundreds of years ago. Their **descendants** were living there when in 1493 Christopher Columbus became the first European to reach the island. Columbus claimed the island for Spain, and soon Spaniards had established a settlement there.

Puerto Rico was a Spanish colony for almost four centuries. At the end of the 1800s, the United States defeated Spain in the Spanish-American War. Afterward the island was turned over to the United States. In 1951 the island became a commonwealth. Some people on the island want it to become a U.S. state, but in elections most of the people have voted against this.

LEARN MORE! READ THESE ARTICLES...
ISLANDS (VOLUME 1) • SPAIN (VOLUME 6)
UNITED STATES: A WEALTH OF RESOURCES
AND BEAUTY (VOLUME 9)

SEARCH LIGHT

True or false? Puerto Rico is one of the 50 states of the United States.

Answer: FALSE. Puerto Rico is an American commonwealth.

More than 2 million people live in Havana,
Cuba's capital city.

SEARCH LIGHT

True
or false?
Cuba is
ruled by Spain.

Sugarcane and Politics

The country of Cuba is part of the West Indies, a group of islands in the Caribbean Sea. The country is made up of one main island and about 1,600 smaller islands. The capital is Havana, on the north-western coast of the main island.

Havana

Many Cubans are farmers. For a long time the most valuable crop has been sugarcane. Sugarcane grows as a tall, thick grass, and it is from this plant that we get sugar. Cuba also produces tobacco, and Cuban cigars are famous worldwide. Other major crops are coffee, rice, and tropical fruits. Although making sugar from cane is still important, many factories have been closed. Tourism is now the largest source of income for Cuba.

Cubans speak Spanish, and the country's culture reflects its Spanish background. The island was claimed for Spain by Christopher Columbus in 1492 and was ruled by Spain until the 1890s. African culture has also influenced Cuba. Many Africans were taken to the island long ago to work as slaves on the sugar plantations.

Cuba saw major changes when Fidel Castro took over the government in 1959. Castro was strongly **communist**, and he developed a close relationship with the government of the Soviet Union. This caused problems between Cuba and its neighbour the United States, since the United States strongly disagreed with the political ideas of the Soviet Union. In fact, Cuba was nearly the centre of a nuclear war between the United States and the Soviet Union in 1962. The problems remained even after the Soviet Union collapsed in 1991.

LEARN MORE! READ THESE ARTICLES...
FIDEL CASTRO (VOLUME 4) • SUGARCANE (VOLUME 10)
WEST INDIES (VOLUME 9)

DID YOU KNOW?

Large stalks of sugarcane are often sold in fruit markets in Cuba. For children it's a treat to have a small section of sugarcane to suck on, like an ice lolly.

Answer: FALSE. Cuba was ruled by Spain for many years but gained independence in the 1890s.

The bright green emerald tree boa is native to the Amazon Basin of South America.
© David A. Northcott/Corbis

13

5

11

8   7

6

10

2

3

9

1

12

Rio de Janeiro, Brazil.
© Richard T. Nowitz/Corbis

The Unknown Continent

Scientists believe that millions of years ago South America and Africa were part of the same ancient **landmass** now known as Gondwanaland. In fact, if you view South America and Africa as puzzle pieces, you'd see that the two continents fit roughly together. Slowly, South America broke away and began to drift westward. Today the **Isthmus** of Panama links South America to North America. The South American mainland is divided into 12 independent countries and one dependent state.

The Andes Mountains, one of the longest and highest mountain ranges in the world, lie in South America. The continent also features the Guiana Highlands and the Brazilian Highlands, which contain some of the oldest rocks on Earth. The River Amazon in South America is one of the greatest rivers of the world. A huge quantity of the world's freshwater flows through the Amazon **basin**. The river makes the **lush** Amazon rainforest possible.

For thousands of years South America was **isolated** from the rest of the world. Outsiders didn't know about ancient peoples such as the Inca who lived on that continent. Then in 1498 Christopher Columbus landed in South America. Spanish and Portuguese **colonizers** and adventurers followed. They **converted** many of the native Indians to Christianity. Nowadays most South Americans speak Spanish or Portuguese.

South America's many unusual animals - such as llamas, alpacas, jaguars, sloths, and armadillos - were new to the first visiting Europeans. Today many people visit South America to see its rainforests and to enjoy its rich animal life.

COUNTRIES OF SOUTH AMERICA
1. Argentina
2. Bolivia
3. Brazil
4. Chile
5. Colombia
6. Ecuador
7. French Guiana
8. Guyana
9. Paraguay
10. Peru
11. Suriname
12. Uruguay
13. Venezuela

LEARN MORE! READ THESE ARTICLES...
AFRICA (VOLUME 8) • CONTINENTS (VOLUME 1)
NORTH AMERICA (VOLUME 9)

DID YOU KNOW?
Many interesting and important dinosaur fossils have been found in South America. The oldest dinosaur fossil ever found was of Eoraptor, a metre-long dinosaur that lived in Argentina more than 220 million years ago.

Answer: These are all true statements.

The Rainforest River

On a map of South America a thick line cuts across the country of Brazil all the way from the Andes Mountains in Peru to the Atlantic Ocean. That line traces the mighty Amazon River. The other lines that lead into it are major rivers too. Altogether they make up one of the world's greatest river systems, carrying more total water than any other.

Why is the river called 'Amazon'? Many years ago, in 1541, a Spanish soldier named Orellana sailed down the river. He had to fight many women soldiers who lived by the river. It made him think of the Amazons, who were the mighty women soldiers of Greek mythology. So he called the river 'Amazon'.

Along the banks of the river are miles of trees, all tangled together with bushes and vines. This region is known as a 'rainforest'. You can hear the sound of water dripping from leaves because it rains here almost every day. This is the largest tropical rainforest in the world.

In the rainforest there are very tall trees, some as tall as 60 metres. They spread out like giant umbrellas and catch most of the sunlight. There are rubber trees, silk cotton trees, Brazil nut trees, and many others. Many animals, some quite rare, make their homes among the tree branches. These include **exotic** parrots and **mischievous** monkeys - as well as giant hairy spiders!

LEARN MORE! READ THESE ARTICLES…
AMAZON: A CLOSER LOOK (VOLUME 9)
RAINFORESTS (VOLUME 1)
RUBBER TREE (VOLUME 10)

SEARCH LIGHT

True or false? It rains almost every day in the Amazon.

ATLANTIC OCEAN

DID YOU KNOW?

You may hear 'Amazon' used for a totally different thing: Amazon.com or Amazon.co.uk. Perhaps this Internet store wants to be the greatest of its kind, just as the Amazon River is.

Amazon River

Peru

Brazil

SOUTH AMERICA

ATLANTIC OCEAN

Answer: TRUE. The Amazon region is a very wet kind of area known as a 'rainforest'.

A Close Look at River Life

SEARCH LIGHT

Find and correct the error in the following sentence: The Amazon rainforest has many trees, plants, animals, people, and insects.

At the heart of South America lies the Amazon River **basin**. It is nearly as large as the United States, but few people live there. Nonetheless, the area is full of living things. They are all part of a giant **tropical** forest called the rainforest. There are so many plants, animals, birds, and insects there that no one has been able to list them all! Some of them exist nowhere else in the world.

The rainforest is a very important place. It helps control the world's **climate** by absorbing gases in the air that can cause a problem called

Emerald tree boa in the Amazon basin.
© David A. Northcott/Corbis

global warming. It also provides a home for the many animals in the area.

There are brightly coloured birds, including green and yellow parrots with red heads, pink flamingos, and beautiful hummingbirds. There are also millions of butterflies, some as big as small birds.

The treetops are alive with playful monkeys. On the ground are funny-looking animals called tapirs that resemble hairy pigs. There are also animals that you wouldn't enjoy meeting. The spotted jaguar, a large member of the cat family, is one. The anaconda is another. It is one of the world's largest snakes and can swallow a whole deer in one gulp! There are also huge hairy spiders, many-legged centipedes, and army ants that eat almost everything that they find.

It's not a good idea to swim in the Amazon River. What looks like a floating log might actually be a dangerous crocodile. There are electric eels that can hurt a person with an electric shock. And there are harmless-looking fish called piranhas that are actually quite ferocious, though they don't usually bother people.

LEARN MORE! READ THESE ARTICLES...
NILE RIVER (VOLUME 8) • RAINFORESTS (VOLUME 1) • RIVERS (VOLUME 1)

The Amazon is home to many different types of wildlife, including the green-cheeked Amazon parrot.
© Eric and David Hosking/Corbis

Answer: The Amazon rainforest has many trees, plants, animals, birds, and insects.

World-Class Mountains

The Andes are the tallest mountains in the Western **Hemisphere**. The highest peak, Mount Aconcagua in Argentina, is about 6,960 metres high. The mountains run north to south for the entire length of South America - 8,900 kilometres in all. They separate a narrow strip of land along the west coast from the rest of the continent.

The Andes region is made up of many high **plateaus** surrounded by even higher peaks. In some sections, the chain separates into two ranges. The Cordillera Oriental is the eastern mountain range, and the Cordillera Occidental is the western range.

Andean condors.
© Galen Rowell/Corbis

Because of the extreme **altitudes**, the mountains can be a very difficult place to live. There are few plants above 4,900 metres, but between 2,400 and 3,500 metres there is plenty of good farming. This is the zone where most of the people of the Andes live and where most of the cities are. Just above this zone is where llamas and alpacas are raised. These relatives of the camel are valuable for their wool and for other purposes. At higher elevations there is less oxygen to breathe. Few people live at heights greater than 3,700 metres. Sheepherders, though, sometimes live as high as 5,000 metres.

The best-known people ever to live in the Andes were the Inca. When Europeans arrived in the mountains in the 1500s, the Inca ruled much of the area. Remains of the magnificent Inca city called Machu Picchu can still be seen in the mountains of Peru.

LEARN MORE! READ THESE ARTICLES…
LLAMAS (VOLUME 12) • MACHU PICCHU (VOLUME 9)
MOUNTAINS (VOLUME 1)

SEARCH LIGHT

Mount Everest, the world's highest mountain, is over 8,800 metres tall. How much taller than Mount Aconcagua is it?
a) about 180 metres
b) about 4,880 metres
c) about 1,830 metres

Mount Fitzroy and Mount Torre belong to the part of the Andes Mountains in south-western Argentina. Altogether, the Andes Mountains pass through seven different countries in South America.
© Francesc Muntada/Corbis

DID YOU KNOW?

Andean condors are among the largest flying birds on Earth. Their wings measure 3 metres across from tip to tip and are strong enough to allow these giants to fly as many as 320 kilometres a day looking for food.

The Islands at the End of the World

A tortoise as big as a bathtub!

Giant lizards that look like dragons!

These are only a few of the special things that make the Galapagos Islands different from any other place on Earth. The islands lie in the Pacific Ocean, far away from any other land. People have called them 'the world's end'. Like some other natural wonders, the Galapagos have been named a World Heritage site.

The Galapagos Islands were formed from volcanoes that erupted in the sea. The bare and rocky islands look as if no creature could ever live there. But thousands of animals do, including many found nowhere else in the world. One animal that lives there is the giant tortoise, or land turtle. In fact, the islands got their name from these tortoises. The word *galápagos* means 'tortoises' in Spanish.

One of the many varieties of finches on the Galapagos Islands.
© Galen Rowell/Corbis

The Galapagos Islands were especially important to the famous British scientist Charles Darwin. When Darwin visited the islands, he discovered that there were creatures living there that did not live anywhere else in the world. He saw metre-long lizards - land iguanas that looked like small dragons. And he saw amazing **marine** iguanas - lizards that had actually learned to swim. He also found a great many birds called 'finches' that were all much the same except for differences in their beaks. These differences meant that they all ate different things, which allowed them all to share the same **habitat**.

Darwin decided that all plants and animals evolve, or change little by little, as the world around them changes. One plant or animal group will usually be more successful than another. Darwin called this process 'natural selection'. And he called the overall change through time the 'theory of evolution'.

Do you think people are evolving? What do you think we might look like in a million years?

LEARN MORE! READ THESE ARTICLES...
CHARLES DARWIN (VOLUME 4) • ISLANDS (VOLUME 1) • TURTLES (VOLUME 11)

The giant Galapagos tortoise can live as long as 150 years - longer than almost any other animal. Sadly, few are left today.
© Craig Lovell/Corbis

SEARCH LIGHT

Darwin's famous theory is called
a) natural selection.
b) good versus evil.
c) the big bang.

DID YOU KNOW?

The Galapagos finches all developed from the same ancestor. But to share such a small area, different groups developed beaks suited to different feeding habits. This fact helped Darwin understand how species change.

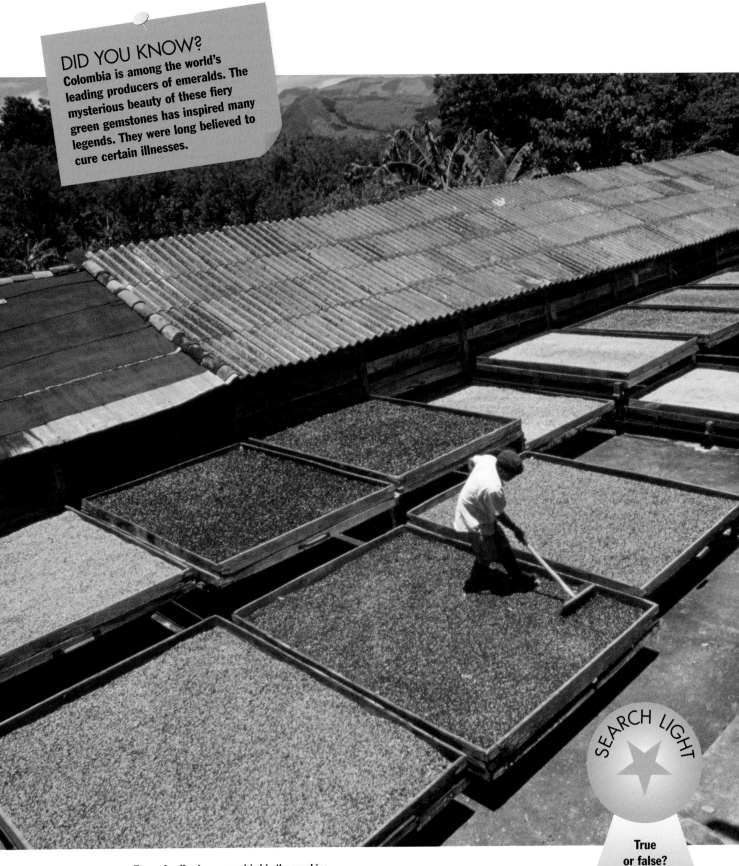

Trays of coffee beans are dried in the sunshine on the roof of a farm building in north-western Colombia. Colombia grows much of the world's supply of coffee beans.
© Jeremy Horner/Corbis

SEARCH LIGHT

True or false? There are more kinds of birds found in Colombia than in all of North America.

Columbus' South American Namesake

Colombia, in South America, is the only American nation named for Christopher Columbus. Its capital city, Bogotá, sits on a high **plateau** in the Andes Mountains.

Colombia is a land of beaches, deserts, jungles, grasslands, and mountains. The Andes range runs the length of the country. Southeast of the mountains, rivers crisscross the lush green Amazon rainforest. In the east are grasslands called the Llanos.

Since Colombia lies close to the **equator**, its climate is generally hot. But it's cooler in the highlands. The rainforest gets more than 250 centimetres of rain annually. The Llanos region has dry and wet seasons.

Colombia is home to many different kinds of plant and animal. There are more than 130,000 different plants in the country, including a kind of water lily called *Victoria amazonica*. Its leaves are large and strong enough to support a child. Just some of the animals found in Colombia include jaguars, ocelots, peccaries, tapirs, deer, anteaters, monkeys, and the rare spectacled bear. There are more than 1,550 kinds of birds in Colombia. That's more than Europe and North America have combined. These birds include the huge Andean condor and the tiny hummingbird.

Bogotá

Before the Spaniards landed in the area in the 1500s, there were many Indian tribes living there. They crafted gold and made stone sculptures. The Spaniards took the people's lands and made them slaves. Many other Indians died of disease. Finally, the people **revolted**, and Colombia became free in 1813. Spanish is still the official language of Colombia.

LEARN MORE! READ THESE ARTICLES...
BIRDS (VOLUME 11) • BOGOTÁ, COLOMBIA (VOLUME 9)
TAPIRS (VOLUME 12)

Answer: TRUE. Colombia has more kinds of birds than Europe and North America have combined.

SEARCH LIGHT

What happened in 1920 to connect Bogotá more closely with the rest of the world?

Capital City of Churches

The city of Bogotá is the capital of Colombia, in South America. Bogotá is located on a sloping plain at the base of two mountains, Monserrate and Guadalupe. Monserrate is a traditional symbol of the city. People believe that it is a place of miracles. At the **crest** of each mountain is a large church. Within the city are many more churches. Most of Bogotá's churches were built by the Spanish.

Before the Spanish arrived in Colombia, Chibcha Indians lived in the area where Bogotá now stands. The Chibcha called it Bacatá. The Spanish conquered the Chibcha and founded the city of Bogotá in 1538. It was not until the early 1800s that Simón Bolívar freed Colombia and its neighbours from the Spanish.

In 1821 Bogotá became the capital of Gran Colombia. This was a union of the present countries of Venezuela, Ecuador, Panama, and Colombia. The countries later separated, and Bogotá became the capital of New Granada. Later New Granada became the Republic of Colombia.

Although Bogotá was the capital of the country, it remained cut off from the rest of the world for a long time. Its location among such high mountains made it very difficult for people to travel in and out of the city. But that changed after an air service was started in the city in 1920. The service connected the city with the rest of Colombia and with other countries. Today many people visit Bogotá to see its churches and its beautiful old buildings.

People feeding pigeons in front of a church in Bogotá's Plaza Bolívar.
© Carl & Ann Purcell/Corbis

LEARN MORE! READ THESE ARTICLES...
AIRPLANES (VOLUME 2) • SIMÓN BOLÍVAR (VOLUME 4)
COLOMBIA (VOLUME 9)

DID YOU KNOW?
People like to visit the church atop Monserrate. But it's a long way up - roughly 550 metres! Some visitors climb up, but many prefer to take the little cable car that runs to the top.

Aerial cable cars carry visitors up Monserrate mountain on the outskirts of Bogotá, Colombia.
© Carl & Ann Purcell/Corbis

Answer: The city's first air service began in 1920. This meant that people could travel to and from Bogotá much more easily than before.

A Peruvian girl displays
a style of traditional dress
that is still worn among some
of the country's inhabitants.

SEARCH LIGHT

Unscramble
these words
having to do
with Peru.
- deAns
- caln
- mazonA

Land of the Inca

Peru is a large South American country that lies just south of the **equator**. In the west it has a long coastline on the Pacific Ocean. Many of Peru's major cities are located on a narrow strip of flat land along the coast. Among them is Lima, the capital. Eastern Peru is part of the huge **basin** of the Amazon River. It is nearly covered with rainforests. Between the coast and the Amazon region are the Andes. Some peaks in this mountain range reach higher than 3,000 metres. High in the Andes is Lake Titicaca, one of the largest lakes in South America.

Around AD 1200 a group of Indians called the Inca formed the city of Cuzco in what is now Peru. From there they set out to conquer other Indian peoples along South America's west coast. Eventually the Inca ruled over as many as 12 million people. But their great **empire** was destroyed when Spanish soldiers seized the land in the 1530s. Spain ruled until Peru won its independence almost 300 years later.

Today Peru still has many reminders of the Inca. The country's name comes from a word meaning 'land of abundance' in Quechua, the Inca language. The name refers to the riches that the Inca got from the land, including great amounts of gold. Indians who still speak the Quechua language make up about half of Peru's population. And in the Andes there is Machu Picchu. The remarkable stone remains of this Inca settlement attract visitors from all over the world.

LEARN MORE! READ THESE ARTICLES...
ANDES (VOLUME 9) • MACHU PICCHU (VOLUME 9)
RAINFORESTS (VOLUME 1)

> **DID YOU KNOW?**
> Peru is known for two domesticated animals that are native to the Andes, llamas and alpacas. These animals are surefooted climbers well suited for life in the mountains.

Lima

Answer: deáns = Andes
caín = Inca
mazonA = Amazon

For hundreds of years Machu Picchu was known only to a few people who lived nearby. The rest of the world learned about the site only when an archaeologist named Hiram Bingham discovered it in 1911.

SEARCH LIGHT

Why did the Inca abandon Machu Picchu?

Secret of the Andes

Along time ago, a group of people who worshipped the Sun lived in South America. They constructed incredible stone buildings high in the Andes, a chain of mountains in the western part of the continent. These people were the Inca. Their most famous creation was Machu Picchu, in the mountains of Peru.

The Inca ruled a large **empire** and had a lot of gold. Their fame reached far and wide. Even the rulers of Spain heard about their 'land of gold'. In the 1500s the Spanish invaded the Inca empire. The invaders killed many people, took their gold, and destroyed their religious buildings. The Spanish invasion brought an end to the Inca empire.

Although the Inca had no written records, they left behind **archaeological** clues about their lifestyle. One big clue is Machu Picchu. At some point the Inca **abandoned** the site. No one is sure why. Some people think it's because the site didn't have enough water. After Machu Picchu was abandoned, trees and plants grew over it. This kept it hidden from the Spanish during their invasion. The site remained unknown to people outside of the Andes until an archaeologist found it in 1911.

If you visit Machu Picchu, you'll find great temples and palaces. You'll also see dozens of stepped **terraces** for farming all around the site. There are also a plaza (square), houses, and a cemetery. Walkways and thousands of stone steps connect the different parts of the site. These structures were probably built in the 1400s and 1500s. But amazingly, almost all of them are still in very good shape. The Inca must have been some builders!

Religious centre, Machu Picchu.
© Craig Lovell/Corbis

DID YOU KNOW?

The name Machu Picchu means 'old peak' in Quechua, the language of the Inca.

LEARN MORE! READ THESE ARTICLES…
ANGKOR WAT (VOLUME 7) • MAYAN CIVILIZATION (VOLUME 4) • PERU (VOLUME 9)

© Jim Zuckerman/Corbis

Answer: It's still not certain, but it could have been because of a lack of water.

Rio de Janeiro is the second largest city in Brazil. It is located on the Atlantic Ocean in the south-eastern part of the country.
© Richard T. Nowitz/Corbis

SEARCH LIGHT

Which of the following can be said of Brazil? It makes up half of South America. It's named for a tree. The national sport is basketball. The Nile River is in Brazil.

Half of South America

★ Brasília

Brazil, the largest country in South America, took its name from brazilwood. The first European settlers in Brazil shipped a lot of brazilwood back to Europe, where it was used to produce valuable red dyes.

Brazil covers nearly half of the continent. It has a long coastline along the Atlantic Ocean. It shares borders with every South American country except Chile and Ecuador. The capital of Brazil is Brasília. Two other Brazilian cities - São Paulo and Rio de Janeiro - rank among the world's largest. Both of these cities lie on the coast. The River Amazon is a key natural feature of Brazil. It is the largest river in the world in terms of the amount of water it carries. More than 1,000 tributaries, or smaller rivers, empty into the Amazon. During the river's annual flood, it pours more than 174 million litres of water per second into the Atlantic Ocean.

The lush Amazon rainforest covers much of the river's huge **basin**. This rainforest contains the most varied plant life on Earth. Nearly 50,000 kinds of animal are also found there. So many different kinds of plant and animal live in the forest that many of them haven't been named yet!

Brazil's national sport is football. The Brazilian team has won the World Cup soccer championship five times. Pelé, a Brazilian national hero, is considered to be one of the greatest soccer players ever.

LEARN MORE! READ THESE ARTICLES...
AMAZON: THE RAINFOREST RIVER (VOLUME 9)
BRASÍLIA, BRAZIL (VOLUME 9)
PELÉ (VOLUME 4)

DID YOU KNOW?
The large and gentle monkey called the 'muriqui' is found only in the eastern forests of Brazil. It is one of the world's most endangered animals.

Answer: It makes up half of South America, and it's named for a tree.

SEARCH LIGHT ★

Which of these sights is not in Brasília?
a) the Congressional Palace
b) the Palace of the Dawn
c) Buckingham Palace
d) the Square of Three Powers

DID YOU KNOW?

Brasília is not the only city built to serve as a national capital. Washington, D.C., was planned and built as the U.S. capital around 1800. Other planned capitals include Canberra, Australia, and Islamabad, Pakistan.

A Bow, a Bird, an Airplane

Brasília is the capital of Brazil, the largest country in South America. The city lies on a **plateau** in central Brazil, near the starting point of three rivers, the Tocantins, the Paraná, and the São Francisco.

Brasília was planned and built in the 1950s to replace Rio de Janeiro as

Four large statues known as the Four Evangelists at the entrance to the Catedral Metropolitana in Brasília.
© Jeremy Horner/Corbis

Brazil's capital. Brazilian **architect** Lucio Costa designed the city in a shape that reminded many people of a bird, a bow and arrow, or even an airplane! He arranged its neighbourhoods around large groups of blocks of flats called 'superblocks'. Each superblock also contains schools, shops, and open parks.

The Square of Three Powers marks the centre of Brasília. Around it you'll see the important government

buildings. Oscar Niemeyer, another Brazilian architect, designed these buildings, which include the striking Congressional Palace. It has twin towers with a large white dome on one side. The dome is where the **Senate** meets. On the other side of the towers is a huge bowl-like structure that houses the Chamber of **Deputies**. Also in the square are the Palace of the **Supreme Court** and the Planalto Palace, where the president's office is located.

Near the Square of Three Powers is Lake Paranoá. At the northern and southern ends of the lake are fashionable neighbourhoods that are quite separate from the central part of the city. Both are full of hotels, restaurants, cafés, and clubs. On a triangular piece of land jutting into the middle of the lake stands the Palace of the Dawn, the president's home.

LEARN MORE! READ THESE ARTICLES…
ARCHITECTURE (VOLUME 3) • BRAZIL (VOLUME 9)
BUENOS AIRES, ARGENTINA (VOLUME 9)

The Congressional Palace is among the many impressive modern public buildings in downtown Brasília.
© George Holton/Photo Researchers, Inc.

Answer: c). Buckingham Palace is in London, England.

DID YOU KNOW?
The first people to live in what is now Paraguay were the Guaraní Indians. Today many of Paraguay's people speak two languages - Guaraní and Spanish.

The Once-Forgotten Land

Not long ago nobody knew much about Paraguay, a country in South America. For much of the 1800s and 1900s Paraguay was ruled by **dictators** who kept the country isolated from the rest of the world. But in the 1990s the country began to open up and encourage visitors.

Paraguay is located in the south-central part of South America. Its capital is Asunción. The country is surrounded by land, and rivers provide the only way to get to the Atlantic Ocean. This makes the rivers very important to Paraguay. In fact, the country's name may come from an Indian word meaning 'river that gives birth to the sea'.

SEARCH LIGHT

For a long time most people knew little about Paraguay. Why?

The Paraguay River divides the country into two natural parts. To the east the land is mostly wooded hills and grassy plains. To the west is a dry, flat region called the Chaco Boreal. It is part of the larger Gran Chaco region, which extends into Bolivia and Argentina.

The wild animals of Paraguay include bats, monkeys, armadillos, anteaters, otters, jaguars, and nutrias, which are rats that can live in water. In the Chaco there are a small number of Chacoan peccaries, which look something like wild pigs. Scientists thought these animals were **extinct** until some living ones were found in the early 1970s.

Asunción ★

The people of Paraguay live mostly in the east. More of them work in farming than in any other kind of job. They grow sugarcane, **cassava**, maize, rice, and tobacco. They also produce a tea called 'yerba maté', which is popular in Paraguay and neighbouring countries.

LEARN MORE! READ THESE ARTICLES…
ASUNCIÓN, PARAGUAY (VOLUME 9) • RIVERS (VOLUME 1) • TEA (VOLUME 10)

Traditional Latino dancing is showcased at an outdoor plaza (square) in Asunción, Paraguay.
© Sarah JH Hubbard/Lonely Planet Images

Answer: Paraguay was run by dictators for much of the 1800s and 1900s. These leaders didn't let the country's people have much contact with people in other countries.

83

Capital of Spanish and Indian Heritage

For many years the Guaraní Indians lived a simple life in Paraguay. They fished, trapped small animals, and did a little farming to survive. They

The Catedral Metropolitana in the heart of Asunción.
© Donald C. & Priscilla Alexander Eastman /Lonely Planet Images

were friendly and peaceful. When the Spanish arrived in 1537, they set up a base at Asunción. They **converted** the Guaraní to Christianity. In time, many Spanish and Guaraní people married. Most of the Paraguayan people of today have mixed Spanish and Indian origins.

Under Spanish rule, Asunción grew into a city. The Spanish built a cathedral and a textile mill. They also used the city as a base for military expeditions to other South American countries, such as Colombia, Peru, and Brazil. But the people of Paraguay longed to be free of Spanish rule. In 1811 they declared their independence.

Today Asunción is Paraguay's capital and largest city. And because it is located on the Paraguay River, Asunción is an important centre for trade. In the city centre there are tall modern buildings. But in other parts of the city you can still see buildings from Asunción's **colonial** history.

If you visit Asunción, you should see the old cathedral. It's called the Casa Viola and is now a museum. You should also visit the presidential palace, the Palacio de Gobierno. The liveliest time to be in Asunción is February. That is when the people celebrate Carnival, a street festival of dance, music, food, and parades. Many people dress in fantastic costumes and masks for the celebration.

SEARCH LIGHT

Find and correct the error in the following sentence: February is the liveliest time to be in Asunción because that is when the people celebrate the Harvest.

LEARN MORE! READ THESE ARTICLES...
BRASÍLIA, BRAZIL (VOLUME 9) • BUENOS AIRES, ARGENTINA (VOLUME 9)
MARY (VOLUME 5)

A statue guards the entrance to Asunción's Congressional Palace.
© Donald C. & Priscilla Alexander Eastman/Lonely Planet Images

Answer: February is the liveliest time to be in Asunción because that is when the people celebrate Carnival.

85

A Long and Narrow Land

No other country has a shape like Chile's. The country stretches along South America's Pacific coast for a long 4,300 kilometres but is only a skinny 180 kilometres wide. Chile controls Easter Island in the Pacific and claims part of Antarctica as well. Its capital is Santiago.

Most of Chile is dominated by the Andes Mountains. Many people there raise llamas and alpacas for wool. But the country is so long that it has many habitats other than the **alpine**. The north is mainly desert. Some **cacti** and shrubs grow there. Central Chile is **temperate** and has land that's good for farming. Most of Chile's people live there. The area is known for its unique *matorral* habitat, with mixed trees, shrubs, cacti, and grass. But people have cleared away much of this growth for firewood. Very few people live in the far south. There are grasslands suitable

SEARCH LIGHT

Fill in the gap:
Chile is about
_____
longer than it is wide.
a) two and a half times
b) 250 times
c) 25 times

Llamas graze near a snow-capped volcano in northern Chile. People use llamas to carry things. Llamas are also used as a source of food, wool, and hides.
© Graham Neden–Ecoscene/Corbis

for raising **livestock** in the area called Chilean Patagonia. But most of the region is rugged and quite cold.

Chile faces many kinds of natural disasters, including volcanic eruptions, earthquakes, and **tsunamis**. In the winter there are fierce storms and floods. Summer often brings **drought**.

Like much of South America, Chile was **colonized** by Spain in the 1500s. The country won independence in the early 1800s. But the long period of Spanish rule had a lasting effect. Most Chileans are mestizos, a mix of Spanish and American Indian ancestry. And most people speak Spanish.

LEARN MORE! READ THESE ARTICLES...
ISABEL ALLENDE (VOLUME 4) • EASTER ISLAND (VOLUME 9)
LLAMAS (VOLUME 12)

★ Santiago

DID YOU KNOW?
The Atacama Desert in northern Chile is perhaps the driest place on Earth. Some parts of the desert have not had a drop of rain for hundreds of years.

Stone statues called *moai* stand on a slope of Rano Raraku, a volcano on Easter Island.

SEARCH LIGHT

How did Easter Island get its name?

Land of Giants

A line of *moai* statues.
G. Renner/Robert Harding Picture Library

Easter Island is located in the eastern part of the Pacific Ocean. The people who live on the island call it Rapa Nui. But the first European visitors to land there, the Dutch, named it Paaseiland, meaning 'Easter Island', because they arrived on Easter Sunday. Today Easter Island is a part of the South American country of Chile.

Easter Island is only 23 kilometres long and 11 kilometres wide. It lies 3,500 kilometres west of Chile. Although the island is small and isolated, it is famous throughout the world for its huge stone statues of people. They are called *moai*. There are more than 600 *moai* on the island. They stand on giant stone platforms called *ahu*s. Some of the *ahu*s have as many as a dozen statues.

All of the *moai* were carved after about AD 700. Some of them have rounded heads and stubby bodies. One famous *moai* is a lifelike figure of a kneeling man. The statues made at a later date are very tall and slim. These *moai* have a huge **topknot** called a *pukao* on the top of their heads. Most of them are between 3 and 6 metres tall. One statue from this period is almost 10 metres high. It is made from a single block of stone that weighs nearly 74 tonnes. The *pukao* on its head alone weighs about 10 tonnes. One unfinished statue is about 21 metres tall. Its back is still attached to the rock from which it was carved.

DID YOU KNOW?
No one is sure why the Easter Island statues were carved or what they mean. Many people believe that the statues honoured important people who were revered as gods after their death.

LEARN MORE! READ THESE ARTICLES...
CHILE (VOLUME 9) • ISLANDS (VOLUME 1) • SCULPTURE (VOLUME 3)

Answer: The Dutch named the place Paaseiland, meaning 'Easter Island', because they arrived there on Easter Sunday.

Home of the Gaucho

SEARCH LIGHT

Find and correct the mistakes in the following sentence: The first people who lived in Argentina were Spanish immigrants from Europe.

At the southern end of South America lies Argentina, the second largest country on the continent - only Brazil is larger. The capital is Buenos Aires.

The landscape of Argentina is **diverse**, with four main regions. The mountains of the Andes rise in the north-west. The dry Gran Chaco lowlands lie in the north. In the south is the cold dry region of Patagonia. The Pampas grasslands cover the heart of the country.

The Pampas has rich soil and lots of rainfall. It is there that you'll find most of Argentina's farms and ranches. It's also where you'll find gauchos - the famous Argentine cowboys. In the 1700s and 1800s these wandering horsemen hunted large herds of escaped horses and cattle that roamed over the Pampas. Argentine writers celebrated the gauchos in poems and stories. Today the gauchos have a more settled lifestyle, working on the farms and ranches.

The Argentine people are as diverse as the land. The first people who arrived in what is now Argentina were American Indians (Native Americans). They travelled there from North America thousands of years ago. Today most of the population is European. The largest groups are from Spain, Italy, France, Britain, Germany, Poland, and Russia.

Spanish is the national language of Argentina. But because Argentina has so many **immigrants** from different parts of Europe, many other European languages are also spoken. Some Indian languages can be heard as well.

Buenos Aires ★

LEARN MORE! READ THESE ARTICLES...
JORGE LUIS BORGES (VOLUME 3)
BUENOS AIRES, ARGENTINA (VOLUME 9) • CATTLE (VOLUME 12)

Ranchers on horseback drive cattle in Patagonia, the largest region of Argentina.
© Corbis

DID YOU KNOW?

Dance and music are important parts of Argentine culture. The tango, a very dramatic dance, was created in Argentina in the 1800s. Today it is performed all over the world.

Answer: The first people who lived in Argentina were American Indians from North America.

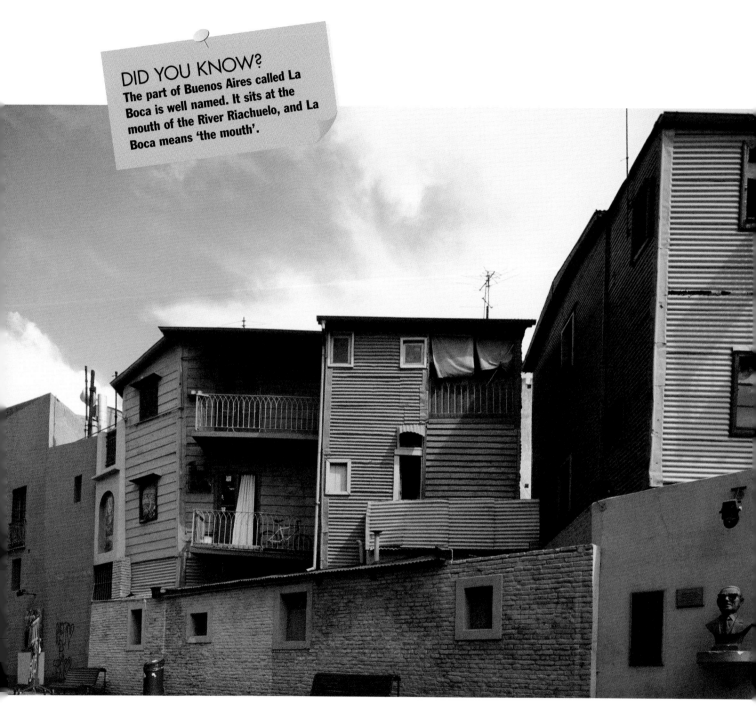

A series of brightly coloured buildings line a street in Buenos Aires, the capital of Argentina.
© Dennis Degnan/Corbis

Argentina's Twice-Founded Capital

Buenos Aires, the capital of Argentina, is one of the world's most important ports and most **populous** cities. Long ago, it is said, Spanish sailors named the port Santa María del Buen Aire for their **patron saint**. The name meant 'Saint Mary of the Good Air'.

Buenos Aires was founded twice. The first time was in 1536 by Spanish settlers. They soon left their new home when they were attacked by local Indians. Almost 50 years later Juan de Garay led a larger expedition back to the site. He refounded the city in 1580.

SEARCH LIGHT

Fill in the gaps: Buenos Aires was founded first in _____ and again in _____.

Skyline of Buenos Aires.
© Pablo Corral V/Corbis

The central section of Buenos Aires still has roads and buildings that were built long ago. The many broad tree-lined avenues in this part of the city date from the 1920s. These roads continue to carry heavy traffic.

A tour of the city usually includes a visit to the tomb of José de San Martín, the hero of Argentina's struggle for independence from Spain. Also popular with tourists is La Boca, a pretty section of the city where the first settlers landed. This was later the site of the city's first meat-salting plants, which made Buenos Aires wealthy in the 1800s. Today La Boca is an artists' colony known for its brightly painted wooden houses.

Visitors to Buenos Aires also enjoy the city's museums and theatres. The Argentine Museum of Natural Sciences has a rich collection of **fossils**. The National Museum of Fine Arts displays the work of great painters from Argentina and all over the world. Buenos Aires is also home to the beautiful Colón Theatre. There you can see outstanding performances of opera, ballet, and classical music.

LEARN MORE! READ THESE ARTICLES...
ARGENTINA (VOLUME 9) • JORGE LUIS BORGES (VOLUME 3)
BRASÍLIA, BRAZIL (VOLUME 9)

Answer: Buenos Aires was founded first in 1536 and again in 1580.

93

G L O S S A R Y

abandon to leave without planning to return

abundance great quantity; plenty

alpine mountainous

altitude the distance of an object above a specific level (such as sea level) on a planet or other heavenly body

ancestry all the family members who lived before a particular individual

archaeology (adjective: archaeological) the science that deals with past human life as shown by fossils, tools, and other material left by ancient peoples

architect person who designs and plans buildings and oversees their construction

basin the area of land drained by a river and its branches

buff an off-white colour

cactus flowering plant of dry regions that has water-storing fleshy stems and, usually, sharp spines

canal artificial waterway for boats or for draining or supplying water to land

cargo goods transported in a ship, airplane, or other vehicle

cassava tropical plant that has a thick underground root-like part and can be made into a number of foods

cathedral large Christian church where a bishop is in charge

château castle or a large country house, especially in France

civilization the way of life of a people at a particular time or place; also, a fairly advanced culture and technology

climate average weather in a particular area

colony (verb: colonize; adjective: colonial) settlement established in a distant territory and controlled by a more powerful and expanding nation

communist follower of a system of government in which all property is owned by the state or community and all citizens are supposed to have a share in the total wealth

congress the main law-making group of some nations

conservation the care and protection of something fragile, unique, and valuable, such as rare wildlife or ancient structures

constitution document containing the basic beliefs and laws of a nation, state, or social group

convert (verb) to win over to a new or different belief

crest in geography, the upper edge or limit of something, such as the top of a mountain

deputy member of a law-making group in some nations

descendant member of a recent age group of a family or similar division that began years earlier

dictator person who rules with total power, often in a cruel or brutal way

diverse varied; different

domesticated tamed

drought long period of dry weather

elevation the height of an object above sea level (that is, the surface of the ocean)

empire a major widespread area under a single government, or a number of territories or peoples under one supreme ruler

engineer person who is trained to design and produce complex structures such as roads, bridges, and dams

equator imaginary circle running east-to-west around the Earth that lies halfway between the North Pole and the South Pole

erosion the process of wearing down; *especially*, the wearing away of soil or rock by wind, water, or ice

exotic unusual and unfamiliar

expedition a planned journey or trip made for a specific purpose

export to carry or send abroad, especially for sale in another country

extend to stretch out or reach across a distance, space, or time

extinct no longer existing

fertile rich and productive; able to yield quality crops in large quantities

fossil an imprint or other trace in rock of an animal, plant, or other living thing

geography the natural physical features of an area; also, the study of the countries of the world and of the Earth's surface features

glacier large river-like body of ice moving slowly down a slope or spreading over a land surface

global warming an increase in the average temperature on the planet Earth

hemisphere half of the planet Earth or any other globe-shaped object

heritage background or descent

hurricane major tropical storm that occurs in the Atlantic Ocean and features high winds moving in circular patterns; in the Pacific Ocean such storms are called 'typhoons'

immigrant person who goes to a country to live there

immigration the process of moving to a new country

isolate to keep separate or alone

isthmus narrow strip of land connecting two larger land areas

landmass large area of land

livestock animals kept or reared, especially farm animals such as cattle, pigs, sheep, goats, and horses

mammal class of warm-blooded animals that feed their young with milk from special mammary glands, have an internal backbone, and are more or less covered with hair

manuscript handwritten or typewritten document

marine having to do with the ocean

mineral substance that is not animal or plant and is an important nutrient for living things

mischievous playfully naughty

natural resources the materials or qualities supplied by nature (such as minerals or water power) that make a place valuable to people, usually for industrial and manufacturing purposes

ocelot medium-sized wildcat of the Americas

organization group of people working together for some purpose

oxygen very common gas that is one of the basic elements necessary for human and animal life

patron saint holy person who is chosen to specially protect a group or place

peccary American animal related to the pig

permanent unchanging, long-lasting, or meant to last forever

petroleum liquid taken from the ground and not yet cleaned or separated into such products as petrol and paraffin; also called 'crude oil'

philharmonic large orchestra that plays classical music

plantation large farming property, usually worked by resident labourers

plateau wide land area with a fairly level surface raised sharply above the land on at least one side

polar region area at or near the North Pole or South Pole

pollute (noun: pollution) to poison or make dirty, often with man-made waste

population all the people living in a country or other specific area

populous having a large population

revere to honour

revolt (verb) to rise up (often violently) against the power of a ruler or government

scenic having to do with a pleasing view or natural landscape

senate official law-making group of some nations

supreme court the highest court in a country or other specific official area

tapered little by little becoming smaller toward one end

tapir hoofed, long-snouted mammal of Malaysia and the Americas that is related to horses and rhinoceroses

temperate having mild weather

terrace area of hillside that has been levelled off to allow farming on the land

terrorist person who uses violence to try to reach political goals

timber wood used for building or carpentry

topknot short mound of hair worn on the top of the head

tropical having to do with the Earth's warmest and most humid (moist) climates

tsunami huge ocean wave produced by an undersea earthquake or volcanic eruption

tundra treeless plain with spotty grasses mostly in extremely cold regions

vast huge or spacious